AMERICAN

TRIVIA

Quiz book

JUST HOW MUCH DO YOU KNOW ?
ABOUT *OUR GREAT NATION*

RICHARD LEDERER
author of *American Trivia*
and *Presidential Trivia*

&

CAROLINE McCULLAGH
author of *American Trivia*

GIBBS SMITH
TO ENRICH AND INSPIRE HUMANKIND

First Edition
18 17 16   5 4 3
Text © 2014 Richard Lederer and Caroline McCullagh

Published by
Gibbs Smith
P.O. Box 667
Layton, Utah 84041

1.800.835.4993 orders
www.gibbs-smith.com

Designed by michelvrana.com
Printed and bound in Hong Kong

Gibbs Smith books are printed on either recycled, 100% post-consumer waste, FSC-certified papers or on paper produced from sustainable PEFC-certified forest/controlled wood source. Learn more at www.pefc.org.

Library of Congress Control Number: 2014939526
ISBN 13: 978-1-4236-3726-4

Dedication

To Jim Wilson, a true student of history
—Richard Lederer

To Roy C. Burge, who taught me to write; Marc J. Swartz,
who taught me to think; and Arn Shein, who taught me to read aloud.
—Caroline McCullagh

Acknowledgment

Thanks to David Feldman.

ALSO BY RICHARD LEDERER

Contents

Introduction

Recent surveys reveal that almost half of Americans don't know that the Constitution gives Congress, and not the president, the right to declare war. One-quarter of Americans say that Columbus set sail after 1750, and one-third can't identify the century in which the Revolutionary War was fought. Three-quarters of respondents do not know that America achieved its independence from Great Britain.

Only 7 percent can name the first four presidents of the United States in order (Washington, Adams, Jefferson, and Madison), and only 21 percent know that the faces of Thomas Jefferson, George Washington, Abraham Lincoln, and Theodore Roosevelt are carved on Mount Rushmore.

While only 25 percent of Americans can identify more than one of the five freedoms guaranteed by the First Amendment of our Bill of Rights (freedom of the press, petition, religion, speech, peaceful assembly), more than half can name at least two members of the Simpsons' cartoon family.

We wrote this book to help make the knowledge of our nation's history at least match the nation's knowledge of *The Simpsons.*

We all share a nation with many people who may look different from us, speak a native language different from ours, pray in a way that may be foreign to us, and dress and eat in ways that we don't. What, then, holds us together in this vast and varied land of ours?

The one thing all Americans have in common is our history. It doesn't matter if you're a first-generation or twelfth-generation American. You own our history. That's what makes you an American. That's the glue that holds us together as a people.

Most of us learn some of that history in school. Then, like so many other facts that we acquired there, the chronicle of our national adventure fades into the background of our lives. Will and Ariel Durant said it best: "We Americans are the best informed people on earth as to the events of the last twenty-four hours. We are not the best informed as to the events of the past sixty centuries."

We hope that the quizzes in this book will make the history of America live for you—that you'll think more about the people who have gone before us and worked so hard to bequeath us a united, spirited, and enchanting country. We hope that you'll find even more precious our national gifts of life, liberty, and the pursuit of happiness.

Any good quiz book consists of items of varying levels of difficulty. Some of the posers in these pages are gimmes. Others are likely to stump you the first time around. Still others—the ones signaled by a —add lightness and humor.

RICHARD LEDERER and
CAROLINE MCCULLAGH
San Diego, California

PRESIDENTS OF THE UNITED STATES

1. *George Washington (1732–1799)*
2. *John Adams (1735–1826)*
3. *Thomas Jefferson (1743–1826)*
4. *James Madison (1751–1836)*
5. *James Monroe (1758–1831)*
6. *John Quincy Adams (1767–1848)*
7. *Andrew Jackson (1767–1845)*
8. *Martin Van Buren (1782–1862)*
9. *William Henry Harrison (1773–1841)*
10. *John Tyler (1790–1862)*
11. *James Polk (1795–1849)*
12. *Zachary Taylor (1784–1850)*
13. *Millard Fillmore (1800–1874)*
14. *Franklin Pierce (1804–1869)*
15. *James Buchanan (1791–1868)*
16. *Abraham Lincoln (1809–1865)*
17. *Andrew Johnson (1808–1875)*
18. *Ulysses S. Grant (1822–1885)*
19. *Rutherford B. Hayes (1822–1893)*
20. *James A. Garfield (1831–1881)*
21. *Chester A. Arthur (1829–1886)*
22. *Grover Cleveland (1837–1908)*
23. *Benjamin Harrison (1833–1901)*
24. *Grover Cleveland (1837–1908)*
25. *William McKinley (1843–1901)*
26. *Theodore Roosevelt (1858–1919)*
27. *William Howard Taft (1857–1930)*
28. *Woodrow Wilson (1856–1924)*
29. *Warren G. Harding (1865–1923)*
30. *Calvin Coolidge (1872–1933)*
31. *Herbert Hoover (1874–1964)*
32. *Franklin D. Roosevelt (1882–1945)*
33. *Harry S. Truman (1884–1972)*
34. *Dwight D. Eisenhower (1890–1969)*
35. *John F. Kennedy (1917–1963)*
36. *Lyndon B. Johnson (1908–1973)*
37. *Richard Nixon (1913–1994)*
38. *Gerald Ford (1913–2006)*
39. *Jimmy Carter (1924–)*
40. *Ronald Reagan (1911–2004)*
41. *George H. W. Bush (1924–)*
42. *Bill Clinton (1946–)*
43. *George W. Bush (1946–)*
44. *Barack Obama (1961–)*

ABRAHAM
LINCOLN

★ ★ ★ ★

The *New York Herald* described **PRESIDENT ABRAHAM LINCOLN** thusly: "Lincoln is the leanest, lankiest, most ungainly mass of legs, arms, and hatchet-face ever strung upon a single frame. He has most unwarrantably abused the privilege which all politicians have of being ugly."

That gangly fellow, who was born in a log cabin and grew up in grinding poverty with little formal education, became what many judge to be our greatest president.

1 One of the best known of American poems begins:

O Captain! my Captain!
*   our fearful trip is done;*
The ship has weathered every rack,
*   the prize we sought is won.*

Who wrote the poem, and what does it commemorate?

2 Who was the first president born in a log cabin?

3 Who is the only American president born in Illinois?

4 What two presidents were born in Kentucky?

5 In 1858, Abraham Lincoln met Stephen A. Douglas in a series of seven debates in their campaigns for senator from Illinois. Who won?

6 Lincoln was born on February 12, 1809. What other famous man was born that day?

7 Who was our first bearded president?

8 What do William H. Seward, Simon Cameron, Salmon P. Chase, and Edward Bates have in common?

9 What is Abraham Lincoln's connection with Thanksgiving?

10 What was different about Lincoln's serving a second term as president?

11 What happened at Lincoln's second inauguration for the first time?

12 Who assassinated Abraham Lincoln and where?

13 What happened to Abraham Lincoln's assassin afterwards?

14 Name the three other presidents who were assassinated while in office.

15 Ever since the assassination of John F. Kennedy on November 22, 1963, historians have pointed out a number of striking similarities between Kennedy's death and Lincoln's. What are some of those coincidences?

16 What had been Abraham Lincoln's philosophy of postwar Reconstruction of the seceded states?

17 On which coin does Lincoln appear?

18 On which bill of currency does Lincoln appear?

19 What do an owl and our sixteenth president have in common? 🐱

20 Which American president is the least guilty? 🐱

Answers

1. This poem by **WALT WHITMAN** commemorates the assassination of the captain of our ship of state, **ABRAHAM LINCOLN**, whom many call our greatest president. Here is the complete first stanza of the poem:

O Captain! my Captain!
*   our fearful trip is done;*
The ship has weathered every rack,
*   the prize we sought is won;*
The port is near, the bells I hear,
*   the people all exulting,*
While follow eyes the steady keel,
*   the vessel grim and daring:*
But O heart! heart! heart!
O the bleeding drops of red,
Where on the deck my Captain lies,
Fallen cold and dead.

2. No, it's not Lincoln. **ANDREW JACKSON** was the first president born in a log cabin, in 1767. Although several more have claimed it, there were only five others—**JAMES BUCHANAN** (1791), **MILLARD FILLMORE** (1800), **ANDREW JOHNSON** (1808), Lincoln (1809), and **JAMES GARFIELD** (1831).

3. Most would answer Abraham Lincoln. It's true that Abraham Lincoln was the first president born outside the original thirteen colonies—but in Hodgenville, Kentucky. Many believe incorrectly that he was born in Illinois. Lincoln spent much of his adult life in Illinois, but our only president who started life there was **RONALD REAGAN** (1911–2004), born in Tampico.

4. Kentucky contributed a president to each side of the Civil War—**ABRAHAM LINCOLN** and **JEFFERSON DAVIS** (1808–1889).

5. Lincoln spoke against slavery; **STEPHEN A. DOUGLAS** spoke in favor. Senators were elected by legislatures at that time, and Douglas won the election. However, Lincoln came to national prominence because of the debates. It positioned him to win the election of 1860 for president.

6. The man whom some called an ape, a baboon, and (impossibly) an ape baboon, was born the same day as **CHARLES DARWIN** (1809–1882), who propounded the theory of evolution.

7. ABRAHAM LINCOLN was our first bearded president. Some say he was responding to a letter from an eleven-year-old girl, Grace Bedell, who suggested that a beard would improve his appearance. **BENJAMIN HARRISON** was the last bearded president and the mustachioed **WILLIAM HOWARD TAFT** the last to sport facial hair. **WILLIAM MCKINLEY** was the only clean-shaven president between Andrew Johnson and Woodrow Wilson. From Abraham Lincoln through Benjamin Harrison, every president to have a beard was a Republican.

8. SEWARD, CAMERON, CHASE, and **BATES** were all members of Lincoln's cabinet, even though they had run against him for the presidency in 1860.

9. In 1863, Lincoln, hoping to unite a sundered nation, issued a proclamation declaring Thanksgiving to be a national holiday to be celebrated on the last Thursday of November. He did this at the urging of **SARAH JOSEPHA HALE** (1788–1879), the prolific author and influential editor of *Godey's Lady's Book* magazine, who wrote the children's rhyme "Mary Had a Little Lamb."

10. Between Andrew Jackson and Abraham Lincoln, eight successive presidents served a single term or less—**MARTIN VAN BUREN** (1837–1841), **WILLIAM HENRY HARRISON** (1841), **JOHN TYLER** (1841–1845), **JAMES POLK** (1845–1849), **ZACHARY TAYLOR** (1849–1850), **MILLARD FILLMORE** (1850–1853), **FRANKLIN PIERCE** (1853–1857), and **JAMES BUCHANAN** (1857–1861).

11. Lincoln's second inauguration marked the first time that African Americans participated in the inaugural parade. Four companies of African American troops and lodges of Odd Fellows and Masons marched.

12. On April 14, 1865, five days after the end of the Civil War, Lincoln was fatally shot by the actor **JOHN WILKES BOOTH** (1838–1865), in Ford's Theatre, located in Washington, D.C.

13. Union troops caught up with Booth at a farm in Bowling Green, Virginia. In the ensuing battle, Booth was shot, and the barn he was hiding in was set ablaze.

14. JAMES GARFIELD was shot on July 2, 1881, and died on September 19 of infection. **WILLIAM McKINLEY** was shot on September 6, 1901, and died on September 14 of gangrene. **JOHN F. KENNEDY** was shot and killed on November 22, 1963.

15. Lincoln and Kennedy repeatedly spoke of having vivid dreams of assassination attempts. Each was warned by advisers not to attend the fatal event.

Lincoln was assassinated in Ford's Theatre, Kennedy in a Ford automobile—a Lincoln. Each was shot on a Friday in the back of the head, each with his wife nearby. Both assassins—**JOHN WILKES BOOTH** and **LEE HARVEY OSWALD**—were known by three names totaling fifteen letters. Neither assassin lived to stand trial.

16. Lincoln's policy is outlined in his second inaugural address. The Union should be reconstructed not with a goal of punishment of the rebellious states but "with malice toward none; with charity for all."

17. The Lincoln penny first appeared in 1909, the first presidential coin.

18. Lincoln appears on the five-dollar bill. It was among the first of the Federal Reserve notes issued in 1914 after that system was authorized by the Federal Reserve Act of 1913.

19. They're both a'blinkin'. 🖐

20. Abraham Lincoln. He's in a cent. 🖐

AFRICAN AMERICANS

★ ★ ★ ★

Some of our ancestors came to the New World to find freedom: freedom of thought, freedom of religion, and freedom from the old shackles of caste and class. Others were transported as slaves. Once here, they didn't wait for freedom; they strove to achieve it.

1 When were the first Africans brought to what would later be the thirteen colonies?

2 Did African Americans fight in the Revolutionary War?

3 Who was **CRISPUS ATTUCKS** (c. 1723–1770)?

4 What did the first official census of the United States, in 1790, show about Africans in the United States?

5 What was the Underground Railroad?

6 What was the Fugitive Slave Act?

Booker T. Washington

7 What was the Dred Scott decision of 1857?

8 What were the Thirteenth, Fourteenth, and Fifteenth Amendments to the United States Constitution?

Sojourner Truth

9 Who was **SOJOURNER TRUTH** (1797–1883)?

10 Who was **HARRIET TUBMAN** (c. 1820–1913)?

11 Who was **BOOKER T. WASHINGTON** (1856–1915)?

12 In 1896, the Supreme Court ruled for Ferguson in the landmark case *Plessy v. Ferguson*. What was this case, and why was it so important?

13 The Niagara Falls Conference took place on the Canadian side of the falls in July 1905. Who attended and why?

14 Who was **THURGOOD MARSHALL** (1908–1993)?

15 Who was **ROSA PARKS** (1913–2005)?

Rosa Parks

Martin Luther King Jr.

16 IN 1983, CONGRESS CREATED A FEDERAL HOLIDAY—THE THIRD MONDAY IN JANUARY—HONORING MARTIN LUTHER KING JR. (1929–1968). WHAT ROLE DID KING PLAY IN THE STRUGGLE FOR CIVIL RIGHTS?

Answers

1. Twenty bound servants (not slaves) were brought from Africa to Virginia in 1619. The importation of servants and slaves (promoted by the Portuguese, the English, and the Dutch) increased slowly during the seventeenth century.

2. An estimated five thousand African Americans, both freemen and slaves, served in the Continental army and state militias or as privateers. At the end of their service, many, but not all, of the enslaved black soldiers received freedom.

3. CRISPUS ATTUCKS, of African and Wampanoag Indian descent, was the first of five men killed at the Boston Massacre on March 5, 1770—the first casualty of the Revolutionary War. Many view him as our first black American hero.

4. In 1790, in a total population of 3,939,625, there were 697,624 slaves and 59,997 free Negroes. Virginia had the highest black population (292,627). New Hampshire had the lowest (157).

5. The Underground Railroad was a system of secret routes and safe houses set up by abolitionists and used by more than ten thousand slaves to escape to free states and Canada. The network was formed in the early nineteenth century and was most active between 1850 and 1860.

6. Passed by Congress on September 18, 1850, as part of the Compromise of 1850 between Southern slave-holding interests and Northern Free-Soilers, the Fugitive Slave Act decreed that all runaway slaves must be returned to their masters.

7. DRED SCOTT (1795–1858) was a slave who sued for his freedom and that of his wife, Harriet, and two daughters, Eliza and Lizzie, arguing that they had lived with their masters in states and territories where slavery was illegal. By a 7–2 majority, the Supreme Court ruled that "any person descended from Africans, whether slave or free" had no claim to freedom or citizenship and thus had no right to bring suit in federal court. The decision nullified Congress's right to regulate slavery in the territories and deepened sectional tensions.

8. The Thirteenth Amendment, adopted in 1865, abolished slavery throughout the United States. The Fourteenth Amendment (1868) defined citizenship for the first time and included former slaves. The Fifteenth Amendment (1870) prohibited denying a citizen the right to vote based on "race, color, or previous condition of servitude."

9. Isabella Baumfree was born a slave in Ulster County, New York. After she was freed when New York outlawed slavery in 1827, she took the name **SOJOURNER TRUTH**. She became an evangelist and social reformer preaching for abolition and women's rights and helping many escaped slaves. In 1864, she visited President Abraham Lincoln in the White House. She also received many posthumous honors. A stamp honoring her was issued in 1986; a Mars probe robotic rover was named after her in 1997; and she was honored with a bust in the U.S. Capitol in 2009.

10. Born a slave, **HARRIET TUBMAN** escaped in 1849 and went to Philadelphia. In 1850, she made the first of nineteen trips south to help more than three hundred slaves, including her parents, escape. These trips put Tubman in danger. If she had been captured, she could have been enslaved again, or she could have been prosecuted under the federal Fugitive Slave Act, which made it a crime to aid a runaway slave.

Dred Scott

11. BOOKER T. WASHINGTON lived the first nine years of his life as a slave. He went on to found Tuskegee Institute (now Tuskegee University) in 1881, and founded the National Negro Business League in 1900, with the help of **ANDREW CARNEGIE**. He became the leading voice for a generation of former slaves and their descendants.

12. The justices, in a vote of 7–1, upheld the doctrine of "separate but equal," legalizing segregation and Jim Crow laws in the United States. This decision stood until 1954, when *Brown v. Board of Education of Topeka* overturned it.

13. Twenty-nine black leaders, including **W. E. B. DU BOIS** and **WILLIAM MONROE TROTTER**, met to create a new national movement for civil rights. They wanted the Niagara Falls Movement to be as strong as the falls for which it was named. The movement failed in 1909 due to continuing conflict between Booker T. Washington and W. E. B. Du Bois, but not before laying the groundwork for the birth of the National Association for the Advancement of Colored People (NAACP).

14. Attorney **THURGOOD MARSHALL** worked for the National Association for the Advancement of Colored People (NAACP) from 1936 to 1961. He represented the NAACP before the Supreme Court in 1954 in *Brown vs. Board of Education of Topeka.* He argued that "separate but equal" was unconstitutional under the Fourteenth Amendment, and the Court agreed with him unanimously. That decision ended racial segregation in the public schools. President Lyndon Johnson appointed Marshall to the Supreme Court. The first African American justice, Thurgood Marshall served from 1967 until his retirement in 1991.

15. In 1955, **ROSA PARKS**, an African American civil rights activist, refused to give up her seat on a public bus to a white man in Montgomery, Alabama. She was arrested for refusing to move to the back of the bus and was fined fourteen dollars. Her act of civil disobedience sparked the Montgomery Bus Boycott led by Martin Luther King Jr. Blacks in Montgomery boycotted buses for more than a year. In 1956, the U.S. Supreme Court declared segregated seating on the city's buses unconstitutional. The boycott ended, but its success encouraged other protests on behalf of civil rights for blacks.

16. MARTIN LUTHER KING JR., an African American Baptist minister, was a leader of the civil rights movement from 1955 until his assassination in 1968, when he was just thirty-nine years of age. He was instrumental in establishing the Southern Christian Leadership Conference, which promoted non-violent demonstrations to protest racial discrimination. A powerful and charismatic orator, King, from the steps of the Lincoln Memorial on August 28, 1963, delivered his "I Have a Dream" speech to more than 220,000 civil rights supporters. Many scholars rank that oration as the most important American speech of the twentieth century. His efforts helped lead to the passing of the Civil Rights Act of 1964 and the Voting Rights Act of 1965. He received the 1964 Nobel Peace Prize.

BENJAMIN
FRANKLIN

★ ★ ★ ★

In Paris in 1783, **BENJAMIN FRANKLIN** (1706–1790) observed the first successful balloon flight. Someone asked him, "What good is it?" Franklin answered, "What good is a newborn baby?"

That was Benjamin Franklin—a towering figure of the eighteenth century who saw a bright potential in everything.

1 IDENTIFY THREE INSTITUTIONS BENJAMIN FRANKLIN STARTED OR IMPROVED THAT STILL IMPACT OUR DAILY LIVES.

2 Benjamin Franklin is the best known of our early inventors. Name some of his inventions.

3 How many patents did Franklin hold?

4 What role did Franklin play in the Revolutionary War?

5 Franklin thought the bald eagle "a bird of bad moral character" because it stole food from other birds. What was his choice for our national bird?

6 What did Franklin's political opponents say to him whenever they got angry at him? 🐢

7 Who invented the grandfather clock? 🐢

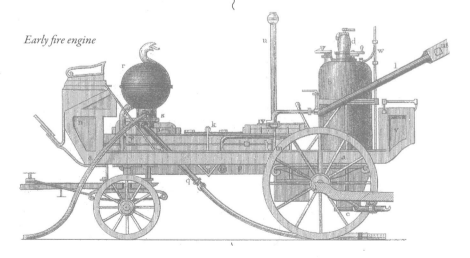

Early fire engine

Answers

1. BENJAMIN FRANKLIN organized the first volunteer fire brigade, reorganized the colonial post office, and established the first free library. He was also the best-known scientist, inventor, statesman, and publisher of his day.

2. He invented the lightning rod, Franklin stove, bifocal glasses, carriage odometer, and the claw pole, used to reach and grasp merchandise on high shelves, among other inventions.

3. Remarkably, Benjamin Franklin refused to patent any of his inventions, preferring to have them used freely as his contribution to the general good.

4. Franklin was our first ambassador to France and helped persuade the French to join with us against the British. He later helped negotiate peace with our adversary, Britain.

Franklin and his stove

5. Franklin favored the wild turkey. The turkey "is in comparison a much more respectable bird . . . though a little vain & silly, a bird of Courage," he wrote in 1784.

6. "Go fly a kite!"

7. Pendulum Franklin.

CHRISTOPHER
COLUMBUS

★ ★ ★ ★

Christopher Columbus (1451–1506) is generally given credit for finding the New World. In grade school most of us learned this ditty:

In fourteen hundred ninety-two,
Columbus sailed the ocean blue.

And he did. On his first voyage, he sighted the Bahamas and made land on Hispaniola (now containing the nations of Haiti and the Dominican Republic). On three subsequent voyages, he also explored the coast of South America. Columbus never realized that he had sailed to the New World. He died in 1506, blissfully certain that he had reached Asia.

Columbus landing at San Salvador, October 1492

1 Who was the first explorer of European descent to set foot in North America?

2 What major differences between the Viking discoveries and **CHRISTOPHER COLUMBUS**'s discoveries led to Columbus being credited with discovering the New World?

3 Name the Spanish monarchs who invested in Christopher Columbus's 1492 voyage to the Indies.

4 Columbus sailed for Spain but was not Spanish. Where was he born? What was his birth name?

5 What were the names of Columbus's three ships on his first voyage to the New World?

6 Where and when did Columbus first set foot on the North American continent?

7 During his four voyages, was Columbus afraid of falling off the edge of the flat Earth?

8 **HOW DO WE KNOW THAT COLUMBUS WAS THE BEST DEALMAKER IN HISTORY?** 😄

9 How did King Ferdinand and Queen Isabella pay for Columbus's voyages? 😄

10 How do we know that Columbus's ships got the best gas mileage in history? 😄

Answers

1. In AD 1000, almost five hundred years before the first voyage of Christopher Columbus, Viking **LEIF ERICSON** became the first European to land in the New World, in Newfoundland, Canada.

2. News of Columbus's discoveries in 1492 had immediate and wide dissemination. Despite earlier rumors, valid evidence of the Viking voyages did not surface until the twentieth century. On his second voyage, Columbus established La Isabela, the first permanent European settlement in the New World.

3. KING FERDINAND and **QUEEN ISABELLA** of Spain backed Columbus's first voyage to the Indies, during which he sailed to the New World.

4. CRISTOFFA COROMBO was born in the Republic of Genoa (now in Italy) in 1451. He began his career as a seaman in the Portuguese merchant marine. Later, in Spain, he was known as Christóbal Colón.

5. The Niña, Pinta, and Santa María, the last of which Columbus captained. Columbus commanded seventeen ships on his second voyage, six on his third, and four ships on his fourth voyage.

6. Columbus never saw North America. He did explore part of the eastern coastline of South America on his third voyage in 1498–1500 and on his fourth and final voyage in 1502–1504.

7. No. Astronomers as far back as the ancient Greeks knew that the Earth was round. **PYTHAGORAS** (c. 570 BC–c. 495 BC) was the first.

8. He left not knowing where he was going. When he got there, he didn't know where he was. When he returned, he didn't know where he'd been. And he did it all on borrowed money. 🐵

9. With their Discover card. 🐵

10. They got three thousand miles per galleon. 🐵

CITIES

The United States boasts the world's most urban population with 83 percent of us living in cities or suburbs, as compared with a worldwide average of 50.5 percent. Since 1990, the number of Americans living in cities has gone up 7 percent. Our ten most populous cities are (1) New York, (2) Los Angeles, (3) Chicago, (4) Houston, (5) Philadelphia, (6) Phoenix, (7) San Antonio, (8) Dallas, (9) San Diego, and (10) San Jose. Following are some questions about our metropolitan clusters, as well as our towns.

Downtown Manhattan, c. 1906

1 WHAT DISTINCTION DOES ORAIBI, ARIZONA, HOLD?

2 What distinction does **ST. AUGUSTINE, FLORIDA**, hold?

3 The fort and other buildings in St. Augustine burned in 1586. What caused the fire?

4 What distinction does **BARROW, ALASKA**, hold?

5 What distinction does **RUGBY, NORTH DAKOTA**, hold?

6 **PHILADELPHIA** is the home of Independence National Historical Park, "America's Most Historic Square Mile." Name some of the landmarks in that park.

7 Which city started the first zoo?

8 Identify the four state capitals that are named for presidents.

9 Which U.S. city is the rainiest?

10 Which U.S. city is the sunniest?

11 Which U. S. city is the least sunny?

12 Which state capital boasts the largest population?

Philadelphia

The Brooklyn Bridge, New York City

17 Identify the cities that have inspired these notable nicknames: (a) the Big Apple, (b) the Windy City, (c) Beantown, (d) the City of Brotherly Love, (e) the Big Easy, (f) the Mile-High City, (g) the Heart of Bluegrass Country, (h) Motown, (i) the Entertainment Capital of the World, (j) Big D, (k) Music City, and (l) the Golden Gate City.

13 NEW YORK CITY is not only our most densely populated city (26,403 people per square mile), it is ethnically rich. How so?

14 PORTLAND, OREGON, could very well have been called Boston. Why?

15 From DETROIT, in what direction would you travel to reach Canada?

16 WHAT IS THE FULL NAME OF LOS ANGELES?

Los Angeles

Answers

1. Founded sometime before AD 1100, **ORAIBI**, a Hopi Indian settlement, is the oldest continuously inhabited village in North America. It's around five hundred years older than St. Augustine, Florida.

2. Founded in 1565 by Spanish explorers, **ST. AUGUSTINE** is the oldest continuously inhabited, European-established city in the continental United States. Spanish treasure ships carried silver from South America to Spain. The Spanish founded St. Augustine as a base to protect these ships from French and English pirates. The settlement also helped them maintain their claim to Florida.

3. English and French privateers and pirates regularly attacked Spanish settlements and ships. **SIR FRANCIS DRAKE**, a privateer commissioned by **QUEEN ELIZABETH I**, set fire to St. Augustine in June 1586. The Spanish rebuilt.

4. **BARROW** (population: 4,200) is the northernmost city in the United States, located three hundred miles north of the Arctic Circle. It's the largest city in the North Slope Borough.

5. **RUGBY** is the geographical center of North America.

6. Among its many landmarks are Independence Hall, where the Declaration of Independence and the Constitution were debated and adopted; Carpenters' Hall, the location of the First Continental Congress in 1774; Christ Church, the home church of **GEORGE WASHINGTON, ROBERT MORRIS, BENJAMIN FRANKLIN,** and **BETSY ROSS**; and the Liberty Bell.

7. The Philadelphia Zoo was chartered in 1859, but the Civil War delayed its opening until 1874.

8. **JEFFERSON CITY, MISSOURI; MADISON, WISCONSIN; JACKSON, MISSISSIPPI**; and **LINCOLN, NEBRASKA**.

9. **HILO, HAWAII**, receives the most rain (annual average: 126.27 inches).

10. **YUMA, ARIZONA**, bakes in the most sun (90 percent of the time). There's a

rumor that Arizona farmers feed their hens crushed ice so that they won't lay hard-boiled eggs.

11. JUNEAU, ALASKA, is visited least by the sun (30 percent of the time).

12. PHOENIX, ARIZONA, with about a million and a half residents.

13. NEW YORK CITY is home to the largest number of Italians outside Italy, the largest number of Irish outside Ireland, the largest number of Jews outside Israel, and the largest number of Puerto Ricans outside Puerto Rico.

Waipio Valley, Hawaii, 1911

14. The city was founded by two New Englanders, one from Maine, the other from Massachusetts. They decided to flip a coin to see who would name the new town: heads, Portland; tails, Boston. The Maine man won the flip.

15. South. **DETROIT** is the only major U.S. city that sits north of Canadian territory.

16. The full name of **LOS ANGELES** is El Pueblo de Nuestra Señora la Reina de los Ángeles de Porciúncula. It can be abbreviated to 3.63 percent of its size: L.A.

17. (a) New York
(b) Chicago
(c) Boston
(d) Philadelphia
(e) New Orleans
(f) Denver
(g) Lexington
(h) Detroit
(i) Los Angeles
(j) Dallas
(k) Nashville
(l) San Francisco

THE CIVIL
WAR

★ ★ ★ ★

It was called the War Between the States, the War Against Northern Aggression, Mr. Lincoln's War, the War for the Union, the Second War of Independence, the Great Rebellion, the War for Abolition, the War for Separation, the War for States' Rights, the War for Southern Independence, and the Civil War.

Whatever you call it, the war that raged from 1861 to 1865 seared our national consciousness and forever changed what it means to be an American.

1 **PRESIDENT ABRAHAM LINCOLN** said to her, "So you're the little woman who wrote the book that made this great war." Who was she?

2 What happened at Harpers Ferry, Virginia, October 16, 1859?

3 On December 20, 1860, by a vote of 159–0, what did the state convention in South Carolina decide to do?

4 Like the first American flag, the Confederate flag ultimately displayed thirteen stars. What did they represent?

5 In 1861, how did new **PRESIDENT ABRAHAM LINCOLN** react to secession and the establishment of the Confederate States of America?

6 Who was **JEFFERSON DAVIS**?

7 Of what significance is Fort Sumter, the island fort in Charleston Harbor, South Carolina?

8 **ABNER DOUBLEDAY** (1819–1893) is erroneously credited with inventing baseball, but he did start a war. How so?

9 As the Civil War broke out, to what Virginian did President Lincoln offer command of the Union army?

10 Who wrote, "I can anticipate no greater calamity for the country than dissolution of the Union"?

11 Virginia's secession on April 17, 1861, gifted the Confederacy with many of the most able U.S. Army officers. Name some of them.

Jefferson Davis

12 WHAT WAS THE "ANACONDA PLAN" THAT GENERAL WINFIELD SCOTT (1786–1866), THE COMMANDING GENERAL OF THE U.S. ARMY, DEVISED TO DEFEAT THE CONFEDERACY?

Winfield Scott

13 The Confederate Navy was vastly overmatched by the Union Navy. To compensate, the Confederate Navy built what kind of new ship?

14 On March 9, 1862, the first-ever battle between ironclads took place in Hampton Roads, Virginia, as the Confederates tried to lift the blockade of Chesapeake Bay. What was the outcome of that clash?

15 How did poet **WALT WHITMAN** (1819–1892) participate in the Civil War?

16 What role did **MATHEW BRADY** (c. 1823–1896) play in the Civil War?

17 What role did humanitarian **DOROTHEA DIX** (1802–1887) play in the Civil War?

Dorothea Dix

18 Of what significance was the First Battle of Bull Run (July 21, 1861)?

19 At the First Battle of Bull Run, Confederate brigade commander **GENERAL THOMAS JACKSON** (1824–1863) earned what nickname?

20 **GENERAL JOSEPH E. JOHNSTON**, the commander of the Confederacy's eastern army, was wounded at Fair Oaks, Virginia, on May 31, 1862. Whom did Jefferson Davis choose to replace him?

21 After the defeat of Union forces at Chickamauga Creek, Tennessee, on September 19–20, 1863, what staff change did **ABRAHAM LINCOLN** implement?

22 A temperance committee asked President Lincoln to fire **GENERAL ULYSSES S. GRANT** because he drank too much. What was Lincoln's reply?

23 In what document did **ABRAHAM LINCOLN** proclaim that "all persons held as slaves . . . shall be then, thenceforward, and forever free"?

24 How did the word *deadline* become part of the English language during the Civil War?

25 Who said, "War is Hell!"?

26 What happened on Palm Sunday, April 9, 1865, at 13:00 hours, in the small settlement of Appomattox Court House, Virginia?

27 How many died in the Civil War?

28 Which six future presidents took part in the Civil War?

29 Through the lens of history, it seems clear that from the outset of the Civil War, the deck was stacked against the South. How?

30 The American Civil War is often referred to as the first modern war. Why?

John Brown

Answers

1. "The little woman" was **HARRIET BEECHER STOWE** (1811–1896), who, in 1851, published *Uncle Tom's Cabin,* an enormously popular and influential antislavery novel that helped mobilize the white North's opinions against slavery.

2. Militant abolitionist **JOHN BROWN** (1800–1859) attacked and occupied the armory building at Harpers Ferry, Virginia. Federal troops commanded by **COLONEL ROBERT E. LEE** (1807–1870) stormed the building and killed ten of Brown's eighteen men. Brown, wounded, was tried within two weeks, and hanged on December 2, 1859. The rhetoric surrounding Brown's assault and death significantly polarized the pro- slavery and antislavery factions.

3. South Carolina became the first state to secede from the Federal Union. By February 1, 1861, the six other states (named below) of the Deep South had followed.

4. The stars represented the seven original Confederate states—South Carolina,

Mississippi, Florida, Alabama, Georgia, Louisiana, and Texas—plus Virginia, Arkansas, Tennessee, North Carolina, Kentucky, and Missouri.

5. Lincoln declared secession void and promised to "hold, occupy, and possess" all government property. In his inaugural address, on March 4, 1861, he avowed that "the Union of these states is perpetual."

6. On February 4, 1861, representatives of the seceded states met in Montgomery, Alabama, to form the Confederate States of America. On February 9, the delegates elected **JEFFERSON DAVIS** provisional president.

7. At 4:30 a.m., April 12, 1861, Confederate forces fired on Fort Sumter. The Civil War had begun.

8. At approximately 7 a.m. on April 12, 1861, in defense of Fort Sumter, **CAPTAIN ABNER DOUBLEDAY** returned fire, the first shot by the Union Army in the Civil War. The Union garrison, lacking ammunition, surrendered the next day.

9. In 1861, Lincoln offered the command to **ROBERT E. LEE**. Lee declined the Union generalship, resigned his U.S. military commission, and ultimately became commander of the Confederate forces.

10. These words, written by **ROBERT E. LEE** before the Civil War, reflect the agonizing decision so many Americans had to make, just as their great-great-grandparents in 1775–1776 had to choose between king and the aborning country.

11. The new Confederacy now included high-caliber commanders **ROBERT E. LEE**, **THOMAS "STONEWALL" JACKSON**, **AMBROSE HILL**, and **JOSEPH JOHNSTON**. The Union army would have a lot of catching up to do.

12. Scott proposed not the invasion of the South, but a series of naval blockades of major ports to obstruct the passage of Confederate supplies. Like an anaconda, these restrictions tightened over time.

13. During the Civil War, the Confederate Navy built more than twenty ironclads, ships that were armored with iron or steel plates. The most famous of these vessels was the CSS *Virginia,* also known as the *Merrimack.*

14. The USS *Monitor* and the CSS *Virginia* pounded each other with cannonballs for almost four hours. The balls bounced off the iron plating, and the duel ended inconclusively.

15. WALT WHITMAN acted as a volunteer nurse and wrote prolifically about his experiences in the conflict.

16. From start to finish of the terrible conflict, **MATHEW BRADY** and his team of camera operators assembled a priceless photographic record of the Civil War. He was the father of photojournalism.

17. DOROTHEA DIX, champion of the mentally ill in the antebellum era, became superintendent of Union nurses at the beginning of the war. More than 3,000 women and men volunteered to work in the Northern hospitals.

18. The two armies clashed near Manassas Junction, Virginia, on a plateau behind Bull Run Creek. In this first major battle of the Civil War, the Union troops were routed. Bull Run awakened people to the possibility that the war was going to be longer and bloodier than first thought.

19. As his brigade stood firm in the face of a Union onslaught, **GENERAL BARNARD BEE** (1824–1861) exhorted his troops with, "There is Jackson standing like a stone wall! Let us determine to die here, and we will conquer!" That's how Thomas Jackson became **"STONEWALL" JACKSON**. Shortly after shouting his famous utterance, General Bee was mortally wounded.

20. JEFFERSON DAVIS chose **ROBERT E. LEE** a day after Johnston was wounded. Lee changed the name of his force of about 70,000 men from the Army of the Potomac to the Army of Northern Virginia.

21. President Lincoln placed **ULYSSES S. GRANT** in charge of all Union armies between the Appalachian Mountains and the Mississippi River, in spite of the concerns of others about Grant's reputation as a drinker.

22. "Well, I wish some of you would tell me the brand of whiskey that Grant drinks. I would like to send a barrel of it to every one of my other generals."

23. These words ring out from the Emancipation Proclamation and took effect on January 1, 1863. The proclamation freed all the slaves in the ten remaining rebellious states, 3.1 million of the 4 million slaves in the United States.

24. *Deadline*, which entered the English language in 1864, began life as a line of demarcation, generally about 17 feet from the inner stockade of a Civil War prison camp, such as Andersonville. Any prisoner crossing this line was shot on sight.

25. WILLIAM TECUMSEH SHERMAN (1820–1891), whose March to the Sea ravaged much of Georgia between November 15 and December 21, 1864, said, "War is Hell!"

26. On that day and time and in that place, **ROBERT E. LEE** surrendered the army of the Confederacy to **ULYSSES S. GRANT**. After four brutal years, the Civil War had ended.

27. Between 650,000 and 850,000 Americans, Northerners and Southerners, were either killed in battle or died of wounds and disease. Yet, so fecund is nature that the U.S. population increased from 31 million in 1860 to 39 million in 1870.

28. ULYSSES S. GRANT, RUTHERFORD B. HAYES, JAMES A. GARFIELD, CHESTER A. ARTHUR, BENJAMIN HARRISON, and **WILLIAM McKINLEY** were all veterans of the Civil War.

29. The Union possessed a vastly greater population, industrial capacity, infrastructure, sea power, food supply, and pool of entrepreneurial talent, all the advantages that a mid-nineteenth-century war required.

30. The Civil War was the first large-scale conflict in which the Industrial Revolution in America played a major role in how the war was fought and who won.

THE COLONIES

★ ★ ★ ★

The first image that may come to your mind when you think of the colonies is that of the Pilgrims: dark clothing, wide white collars, women's white caps, and men's black hats with buckles on the front. But that was only one group. We started the way we have continued, peopled by groups with different origins, cultures, beliefs, and goals—the initial threads in the tapestry that has become America.

1 Between 1492, when **CHRISTOPHER COLUMBUS** made his discoveries, and 1620, when the Pilgrims landed at Plymouth, many explorers and colonists sailed to the Americas. Why?

2 Who was **VIRGINIA DARE**?

3 When **GOVERNOR JOHN WHITE** returned from England to Roanoke in 1590, all 120 colonists were gone. Where did they go and why?

4 Many settlements in the New World failed. What was the first English colony to succeed in what would later be the United States?

5 The settlers at Jamestown set a priceless precedent that we still enjoy today. What was it?

6 In addition to England, what other countries explored and established colonies in North America?

7 Name the areas of North America that the French colonized.

8 The first known use of the term *New England* was in 1616. What was the area known as before then?

9 Name the thirteen original colonies.

10 In 1664, the English forced the Dutch out of New Amsterdam and, a year later, renamed that settlement for the king's brother. What was that name?

New Amsterdam

11 Besides English immigrants, who else came to the thirteen American colonies before 1700?

12 Before slavery was well established in the colonies, labor came from men and women who applied to be indentured servants. What benefits did they derive?

13 Twenty-one people condemned as witches were executed in Salem, Massachusetts, in 1692 and 1693. Was this hysteria unique to that colony?

14 How were those convicted of witchcraft in Salem executed?

15 In 1693, what stopped the Salem witch hysteria and trials?

16 NAME THE FAMOUS PLAYWRIGHT WHO, IN 1953, WROTE A CLASSIC AMERICAN PLAY ABOUT THE WITCH TRIALS OF SALEM.

17 Which college, now a university, was the first in the American colonies?

18 Why were the early American settlers like ants? 🎭

19 Which colonists made the most writing instruments? 🎭

20 What was the favorite dog in colonial times? 🎭

Answers

1. Major powers England, France, Spain, and Portugal claimed territory to exploit the resources of the new lands and to gain naval control of the sea lanes used to ship treasure to Europe.

2. On August 18, 1587, **VIRGINIA DARE**, the granddaughter of **JOHN WHITE**, governor of the Roanoke Colony in what is now North Carolina, became the first English baby born in the New World.

3. No one knows, though there are many theories. They may have died or been killed, but it's possible that the colonists were absorbed by Indian groups as captives or as immigrants.

4. Founded May 13, 1607, the first successful English colony in North America was Jamestown, named for English **KING JAMES I.**

5. Jamestown established a representative government in 1619. Twenty-two delegates from eleven different settlements in the colony were elected to a House of Burgesses, the first elective governing body in a British colony.

6. France, the Netherlands, Spain, Sweden, and Russia all colonized North America at different times. China may have explored the West Coast, but no acceptable historical evidence exists so far.

7. The French established colonies in Florida and Louisiana, including territory up to the Great Plains (later the Louisiana Purchase), as well as in Canada northeast of the Great Lakes.

8. Most Europeans called the area Norumbega. The name was used on maps to designate a possibly mythical native city, a river, and the whole region.

9. The original thirteen colonies, in roughly north-to-south order, were New Hampshire, Massachusetts, Rhode Island, Connecticut, New York, New Jersey, Pennsylvania, Delaware, Maryland, Virginia, North Carolina, South Carolina, and Georgia. Two areas that later became states were not included: Vermont was an independent republic between 1777 and 1791, when it became our fourteenth state, and Maine was a district of Massachusetts until it became our twenty-third state in 1820.

10. New Amsterdam became New York, named after the Duke of York and Albany, later **KING JAMES II**.

11. The thirteen colonies were also settled by the Dutch, Swedes, Welsh, Rhinelanders and Palatines (from areas now in Germany), French Huguenots, Scots, Irish, and Africans (slaves and free).

12. Indentured servants received free passage to the colonies; if they survived to the end of their term of servitude, some received fifty acres of land.

13. Between 1620 and 1723, witchcraft hysteria inflamed other colonies and Europe. While Salem is the most horrific example in America, more than 350 people were accused throughout New England.

14. Fifteen women and five men were hanged. One man was crushed to death with stones. Five years later, one judge, **SAMUEL SEWALL**, confessed his error, and the sentences were posthumously annulled.

15. Most of the accused were poor and socially isolated, but when **MARY PHIPS**, wife of the governor, was accused, **GOVERNOR WILLIAM PHIPS** put an end to the prosecutions.

16. ARTHUR MILLER (1915–2005), Pulitzer Prize–winning author of *Death of a Salesman,* wrote the play *The Crucible,* which he crafted as an allegory of the McCarthyism prevalent in the early 1950s.

17. Harvard, in Cambridge, Massachusetts, was established in 1636 by a bequest from **JOHN HARVARD** (1607–1638), a Puritan minister. He bequeathed his books and half his estate to the school.

18. They lived in colonies.

19. Pencil-vanians.

20. The Yankee poodle.

THE CONSTITUTION

★ ★ ★

The Constitutional Convention began May 25, 1787, in Philadelphia. On September 17, thirty-nine of the fifty-five men in attendance signed our Constitution. **GEORGE WASHINGTON**, as president of the convention, signed first. Then came the representatives of the various states.

They understood the importance of what they had wrought, forging a document that begins: "We the people of the United States, in order to form a more perfect Union, establish justice, insure domestic tranquility, provide for the common defense, promote the general welfare, and secure the blessings of liberty to ourselves and our posterity, do ordain and establish this Constitution for the United States of America."

The United States Constitution is the oldest such written document in use today. It has been the model for constitutions drafted by many other countries.

1 Who is known as the "Father of the Constitution"?

2 What document did the U.S. Constitution replace?

3 What controversies among the states and federal government had to be addressed in the writing of the Constitution?

4 How did the framers of the Constitution address the issue of the balance of power between the small states and the large states?

5 How did the framers of the Constitution limit the power of government and secure the liberty of citizens?

6 How many states had to ratify the Constitution for it to become the law of the land, and how long did that process take?

7 How many amendments are there in the U.S. Constitution?

8 Where would you go to see the original copy of the Constitution?

9 How is a healthy person like the United States?

10 If **JAMES MADISON** were alive today, what would he be famous for?

James Madison

Answers

1. While a member of the Virginia House of Representatives, **JAMES MADISON** was instrumental in creating the Constitution. He also wrote the first ten amendments, called the Bill of Rights. As a result, he became known as the "Father of the Constitution."

2. The Articles of Confederation had been ratified in 1781 to form a framework for government. The members of the Constitutional Convention had meant to revise those articles but soon realized that a whole new document was required.

3. The Constitution set basic rules for the balance of power among governing entities—central government versus states' rights, small states versus large states, and slaveholding states versus free states.

4. They created a bicameral (two-house) legislature. In the House of Representatives, members provide representation for equal numbers of citizens. Senators (two per state) provide equal representation for the states.

5. They created a balance of powers among the executive, the legislative, and the judicial branches of the government. These three divisions create checks and balances among the three functions.

6. On December 7, 1787, Delaware became the first state to ratify the Constitution. New Hampshire, the ninth and last required, ratified on June 21, 1788. In 1790, Rhode Island became the thirteenth state to ratify.

7. Our constitution has twenty-seven amendments. The first ten of those amendments, the Bill of Rights, were proposed by Congress in 1789 and ratified by the states by 1791.

8. The original Declaration of Independence, the Constitution, and the Bill of Rights are all on display in the National Archives in Washington, D.C.

9. They both have good constitutions.

10. Old age.

THE DECLARATION of INDEPENDENCE

The most prominent all-American holiday is the Fourth of July. It's the birthday of our country, and do we ever celebrate! Families gather for parades, picnics, concerts, carnivals, and fireworks. That national outpouring of jubilation commemorates the signing of the Declaration of Independence.

1 Where was the Declaration of Independence signed, and who was its principal author?

2 Which two men signed the Declaration of Independence and later became presidents?

3 The Declaration of Independence guarantees three _____able rights. Fill in the blank and identify the three rights.

4 The Declaration of Independence declares our national sovereignty from which monarch and nation?

5 ON JULY 4, 1776, HOW MANY MEN SIGNED THE DECLARATION OF INDEPENDENCE?

6 **BENJAMIN HARRISON** was a patriot and signer of the Declaration. What special place does he occupy in presidential history?

7 What has feathers, webbed feet, and certain unalienable rights? 🦆

8 Why did the duck shout "Bang!" on the Fourth of July? 🦆

9 Why do Americans like to wear short-sleeved shirts? 🦆

10 Why do Americans give guns to grizzlies? 🦆

Signers of the Declaration of Independence

Answers

1. The Declaration of Independence was signed in the Pennsylvania State House (now Independence Hall) in Philadelphia. **THOMAS JEFFERSON** was the man primarily responsible for crafting the birth certificate of the United States of America.

2. Our second and third presidents, **JOHN ADAMS** and **THOMAS JEFFERSON**, were both signatories of the Declaration.

3. In the Declaration of Independence, the rights of life, liberty, and the pursuit of happiness are **UNALIENABLE** (not *inalienable*).

4. On July 2 (not July 4), 1776, the Continental Congress voted to declare our independence from England and its king, **GEORGE III**.

5. Only two men signed the Declaration of Independence on July 4—**JOHN HANCOCK** (1737–1793) and **CHARLES THOMSON**, the latter as a witness to Hancock's prodigious signature. Most of the rest signed on August 2. Eventually fifty-six delegates signed. Two never did.

6. **BENJAMIN HARRISON** was both the father of **WILLIAM HENRY HARRISON**, our ninth president, and great-grandfather of **BENJAMIN HARRISON**, our twenty-third president.

7. The Ducklaration of Independence. 🦆

8. Because it was a firequacker. 🦆

9. It reminds them of their right to bare arms. 🦆

10. Because we have the right to arm bears. 🦆

EXPLORERS

★ ★ ★ ★

What personal qualities does it take to step off into the unknown? Certainly courage, intelligence, adaptability, and a joy in the doing, no matter the results. Each of the following explorers, and the many others not mentioned, possessed those qualities and more. They expanded the horizons of our nation and our vision.

Lewis and Clark holding a council with Indians

Amerigo Vespucci

3 In 1507, **MARTIN WALDSEEMÜLLER** published the first popular map of the New World and included the name America. Where is this map today?

4 What U.S. National Monument commemorates the achievements of the first European to explore the Pacific Coast of North America?

5 Spaniard **ÁLVAR NÚÑEZ CABEZA DE VACA** (c. 1489–c. 1558) is best known for exploring what area of our country?

1 Why is our country named *America* instead of *Columbia*, even though at the time of naming, many thought that Columbus was the first explorer to land in the New World?

2 THE NAME *AMERICA* WAS DERIVED FROM AMERIGO VESPUCCI'S FIRST NAME. WHAT IS THE ENGLISH EQUIVALENT OF *AMERIGO*?

Henry Hudson

6 Englishman **HENRY HUDSON** (c. 1565–after 1611) is best known for discovering the large bay in northeastern Canada that now bears his name. What other important discovery did he make?

7 In 1803, the United States paid approximately four cents an acre for the Louisiana Purchase. Besides Louisiana, what did it comprise?

8 **PRESIDENT THOMAS JEFFERSON** sent his secretary **CAPTAIN MERIWETHER LEWIS** (1774–1809) and **SECOND LIEUTENANT WILLIAM CLARK** (1770–1838) to explore the Louisiana Purchase and the Oregon region. What did Jefferson expect of them?

9 WHAT DID LEWIS AND CLARK ACCOMPLISH IN THEIR EXPLORATION OF THE LOUISIANA PURCHASE AND THE OREGON REGION?

10 Who discovered Pikes Peak?

Pikes Peak

Answers

1. Italian explorer **AMERIGO VESPUCCI** (1454–1512) wrote about his own voyages (1499–1502) to the New World. **MARTIN WALDSEEMÜLLER** (1470–1522), who drew the first popular map of the New World in 1507, called it *America* to honor Vespucci. He had never heard of Columbus.

2. *Amerigo* is the Italian form of the Medieval Latin name *Emericus,* which in turn issues from the German *Heimirich—Henry* in English.

3. Waldseemüller published 1,000 copies of his map of the New World. The only one known to still exist is housed in the Library of Congress in Washington, D.C.

4. Cabrillo National Monument, in San Diego, honors **JUAN RODRÍGUEZ CABRILLO** (?-1543). He led a flotilla of three ships that brought the first Europeans to California. It's thought he initially touched land at Point Loma, a peninsula that partially forms San Diego Bay.

Juan Rodríguez Cabrillo

5. Cabeza de Vaca and three others were the only survivors among six hundred men sent from Spain to colonize Florida. In traveling from 1528 to 1536 as they looked for a way home, they explored the Gulf Coast from Florida to Texas. Cabeza de Vaca carefully observed the cultures of the American Indian tribes he encountered. In Spain, he wrote from memory the first detailed descriptions of Native American life.

6. In 1609, Hudson sailed up the river in New York now named for him and

traded for furs with Native Americans. Although English, he sailed for the Dutch, and his trip led to the Dutch colonizing New Amsterdam (later New York).

7. The Louisiana Purchase comprised what later became Iowa, Arkansas, Kansas, Missouri, Nebraska, Oklahoma, and parts of Colorado, Louisiana, Minnesota, Montana, New Mexico, North and South Dakota, Texas, and Wyoming, a total of 828,000 square miles. France had hoped to build an empire in North America, but a pending war with Britain and a slave revolt in Haiti changed the plan. President Thomas Jefferson originally intended to buy only New Orleans.

8. Jefferson expected them to study the Indian tribes; describe all birds, trees, plants, flowers, fish, weather systems, and geology; map all interior river systems; and formally claim the land for the United States.

9. Between 1803 and 1806, Lewis and Clark, along with approximately thirty others known as the Corps of Discovery, walked from St. Louis to the Pacific Ocean and back again. They contacted Indian groups, added to scientific knowledge, and proved that one could cross America overland. Their group traveled approximately eight thousand miles, from Missouri to the Pacific Coast and back. The explorers returned to St. Louis in 1806 with maps; specimens and descriptions of plants, animals, and minerals; and information about the peoples of the West, which allowed the United States to establish a better claim to the Oregon region.

10. BRIGADIER GENERAL ZEBULON MONTGOMERY PIKE (1779–1813) led the Pike Expedition that explored the southern part of the Louisiana Purchase, including Colorado, where, in 1806, he found the mountain that was later named after him.

FIRST LADIES

★ ★ ★ ★

What is unusual about the following sentence?

FIRST LADIES RULE THE STATE

AND STATE THE RULE—"LADIES FIRST!"

Perhaps you noticed that the sentence is a palindrome. When read forward and backward word by word, the sentence comes out the same.

Many early first ladies expressed their own preference for how they were addressed. **MARTHA DANDRIDGE CUSTIS WASHINGTON** was often referred to as "Lady Washington." **JULIA TYLER** preferred "Mrs. Presidentress." Others were called "Mrs. President."

The title "First Lady" was first used in a eulogy for **DOLLEY MADISON** in 1849.

Many presidents' wives have not liked the title "First Lady," but this has not stopped them from making their marks on history in diverse ways. Identify each first lady described on the following pages.

Martha Washington

1 She offered her silver service for the first coins minted in the United States.

2 THEY ARE THE ONLY TWO FIRST LADIES WHO HAVE BEEN BOTH THE WIFE OF A PRESIDENT AND THE MOTHER OF ANOTHER PRESIDENT.

3 She often acted as the official hostess during the administration of **THOMAS JEFFERSON**, whose wife Martha had died in 1782, as well as that of her husband, James. She was thus the President's House hostess for sixteen years, an accomplishment unmatched by any other woman in American history. When British troops burned the White House in 1814, she courageously rescued **GILBERT STUART**'s famous portrait of George Washington before she fled the city.

4 During the term of **JAMES BUCHANAN**, our only bachelor

Dolley Madison

president, she, his niece, played the role of first lady.

5 She was the first first lady to have graduated from college. Along with her husband, she banned all forms of profanity, tobacco, and alcohol at presidential gatherings and functions. For this action she earned the nickname "Lemonade Lucy."

6 At the age of twenty-one, she married the forty-nine-year-old bachelor president **GROVER CLEVELAND** in the Blue Room of the White House

and became the youngest of all first ladies. The couple's baby, Esther, was the only child born in the White House to a president. When, in 1889, her husband was voted out of office after his first term, she told the staff to take care of the furniture because they would return. She was right.

7 In 1912, she supervised the planting of the famous Washington cherry trees, a gift from the people of Tokyo.

8 She has been called "the secret president" and "the first woman to run the government." This legend arose from her perceived role in affairs of state after her husband suffered a prolonged and debilitating illness.

9 She broke precedent to hold press conferences, travel to all parts of the country, give lectures and radio broadcasts, and express her opinions candidly in a daily syndicated newspaper column, "My Day."

10 On Valentine's Day, 1962, she offered a tour of the White House on television. Three out of four viewers tuned in to that program, the most watched documentary of television's golden age.

11 She championed the planting of more than a million wildflowers to beautify the nation's highways. She has been called the first conservationist to occupy the White House since Theodore Roosevelt.

12 SHE MARRIED HER HUSBAND IN 1952 AND FIVE YEARS LATER APPEARED OPPOSITE HIM IN THE MOVIE *HELLCATS OF THE NAVY.*

13 She is the only first lady to be elected to high office, as senator from New York. She is also the first first lady to have earned a law degree— from Yale Law School, where she met her future husband. In 1997 she won a Grammy Award for her spoken-word version of her book *It Takes a Village.*

14 She was the second first lady to have earned a law degree—from Harvard Law School, where she met her future husband. At 5 feet 11 inches, she and **ELEANOR ROOSEVELT** are the loftiest of our first ladies.

One of our tallest first ladies

Answers

1. Martha Washington (1731–1802), the first first lady
2. Abigail Adams (1744–1818) and Barbara Bush (1925–)
3. Dolley Madison (1768–1849)
4. Harriet Lane (1830–1903)
5. Lucy Hayes (1831–1889)
6. Frances Folsom (1864–1947)
7. Helen Taft (1861–1943)
8. Edith Wilson (1872–1961)
9. Eleanor Roosevelt (1884–1962)
10. Jacqueline Kennedy (1929–1994)
11. Lady Bird Johnson (1912–2007)
12. Nancy Reagan (1921–)
13. Hillary Rodham Clinton (1947–)
14. Michelle Obama (1964–)

GEOGRAPHY

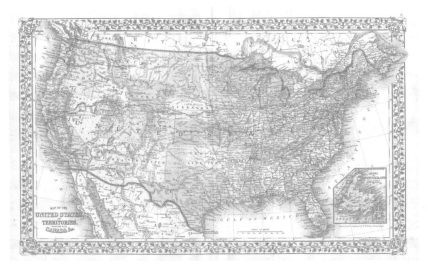

From the redwood forest to the Gulf Stream waters, this land was made for you and me. Many Americans travel all over the world searching for beauty when it exists in their own backyards. Join us for a tour of our homegrown American beauties.

1 Identify the highest point in the United States.

2 The tallest mountain on Earth is in the United States. Which is it?

3 What is distinctive about Mauna Kea's companion, **MAUNA LOA** ("Long Mountain")?

4 What is the lowest point in the United States?

5 Where would you go to encounter the worst weather in the United States?

6 What is the largest river system in the United States?

7 What is the largest body of fresh water in the world?

8 What is distinctive about **CRATER LAKE** in southern Oregon?

9 What is distinctive about **YOSEMITE FALLS**?

Crater Lake, Oregon

10 How accurate is it to call **MINNESOTA** the "Land of 10,000 Lakes"?

11 What is distinctive about the **GREAT SALT LAKE** in Utah?

12 Name two big rivers whose names mean "Big River"?

13 What river, made famous in a Stephen Foster song, originates in the Okefenokee Swamp in Georgia and runs through northern Florida to the Gulf of Mexico?

Answers

1. MOUNT McKINLEY (also known as **DENALI**, an Athabascan name meaning "the high one"), located in south-central Alaska, was renamed in 1896 in honor of President William McKinley. It is the highest point in North America, at 20,237 feet, as remeasured in 2013.

Mount McKinley, Alaska

2. Mount McKinley is dwarfed by **MAUNA KEA**, a dormant volcano on the island of Hawaii. The full name of Mauna Kea is Mauna a Wakea, which means, "mountain that belongs to the sky father, Wakea." Only 13,796 feet high measured from sea level, it is 33,476 feet if measured from its base, taller than Mount Everest (29,035 feet).

3. Only 13,678 feet above sea level, **MAUNA LOA**, as measured from its base, is also taller than Mount Everest. It's the largest volcano in volume and area covered on the Earth. It has been erupting for at least 700,000 years. Since 1832, it has erupted thirty-nine times, the last being in 1984.

4. DEATH VALLEY features the lowest point in the United States, **BADWATER BASIN,** at 282 feet below sea level. Only eighty-five miles separate Badwater from the highest point in the contiguous forty-eight states—**MOUNT WHITNEY**, 14,505 feet above sea level.

5. MOUNT WASHINGTON, NEW HAMP-SHIRE, may have the worst weather in our country. Winds routinely blow at a hundred miles per hour. A gust was measured at 231 mph, the highest wind speed ever recorded in the United States.

6. At 2,323 miles long, the **MISSISSIPPI RIVER** is the largest river system in North America. Along with its major tributary, the **MISSOURI RIVER**, it drains all or part of thirty-one states.

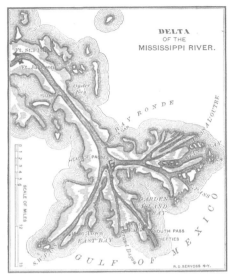

The Mississippi River Delta

9. YOSEMITE FALLS in **YOSEMITE NATIONAL PARK**, at 2,425 feet high, is the highest waterfall in North America and the seventh highest in the world.

10. Pretty accurate. In fact, the state contains 11,840 lakes that are larger than ten acres. **ALASKA** has Minnesota beat, though. There are more than three million natural lakes in Alaska. Only 3,197 are named.

11. The **GREAT SALT LAKE** in landlocked Utah is the largest body of saltwater in the United States. It's so salty that, even in the coldest of Utah winters, it has never frozen over.

12. The **MISSISSIPPI RIVER** (in Algonquian) and the **RIO GRANDE** (in Spanish).

13. The **SWANEE RIVER**. The river is actually the Suwannee. Foster truncated the spelling to make it fit the song called "Old Folks at Home."

7. Canada and the United States share **LAKE SUPERIOR**, the largest body of fresh water in the world.

8. CRATER LAKE is the deepest lake in the United States and the seventh deepest in the world. It was measured by multibeam side-scan sonar in 2000 and was found to be 1,949 feet deep. It sits in the caldera of **MOUNT MAZAMA**, an extinct volcano. Fed only by rainwater and snowmelt, it's one of the clearest lakes in the world.

GEORGE
WASHINGTON

★ ★ ★ ★

GEORGE WASHINGTON, born in 1732, died on December 14, 1799. HENRY "LIGHT-HORSE HARRY" LEE, George Washington's eulogist, said of our first president that he was "first in war, first in peace, and first in the hearts of his countrymen."

Washington crossing the Delaware

1 When did George Washington make his debut in public affairs?

2 By how close a margin was George Washington elected president?

3 What may have been George Washington's greatest gift to the newborn United States of America?

4 George Washington declined an opportunity for a third term as president. What did he recommend in his farewell address in 1796?

5 Who was the first president to appear on a national postage stamp?

6 On what coin does George Washington appear?

7 On what bill of currency does George Washington appear?

8 ON WHAT IMPORTANT MILITARY DECORATION DOES GEORGE WASHINGTON APPEAR?

9 There have been six time spans in American history when no former president was alive. Who was the first president to serve during years when no former president was alive?

10 What far-reaching decision did George Washington have to make about how to cross the Delaware? 😄

11 Having bad teeth, what did our first president wear in his mouth? 😄

12 If George Washington were alive today, why couldn't he throw a silver dollar across the Potomac? 😄

Answers

1. In 1753, before the start of the French and Indian War, **GEORGE WASHINGTON**, a major at age twenty-one, delivered a message to the French near what later became Fort Duquesne (and even later Pittsburgh). The message was that the French should leave the Ohio River Valley. He was rebuffed. His account of his experiences was widely published in America and England.

2. George Washington was the only president to be unanimously elected by the Electoral College, and he did it twice. In 1820, incumbent **JAMES MONROE** won all the electoral votes except one.

3. George Washington might have chosen to become King George I of the United States instead of president, but he had faith in the future of our democracy.

4. Washington warned against the danger of the party system and the entanglements of permanent alliances with foreign nations. He also stressed the importance of a balanced federal budget.

5. The first official U.S. government adhesive postage stamps were issued on July 1, 1847. George Washington was honored on the black ten-cent denomination. **BENJAMIN FRANKLIN**, postmaster general from 1775 to 1776, appeared on the reddish brown five-cent stamp.

6. Washington's profile first appeared on the quarter on August 1, 1932, to commemorate the bicentennial of his birth.

7. Washington first appeared on the one-dollar bill in 1869.

8. Washington's profile appears on the Purple Heart, which had fallen into disuse but was redesigned on the 200th anniversary of Washington's birth (1932).

9. George Washington. There could be no former president alive during the term of our first president.

10. Roe vs. Wade. 🐸

11. The George Washington bridge. 🐸

12. Because a dollar doesn't go as far as it used to. 🐸

THE
GETTYSBURG
ADDRESS

★ ★ ★ ★

The Gettysburg Address contains somewhere between 266 and 273 words, depending on which version you choose. Its brevity partially accounts for the fact that it is the most memorized and memorable speech in American history. Within the brief compass of less than three minutes, a weary president gave a young nation a voice to sing of itself.

Lincoln delivering the Gettysburg Address

Robert E. Lee

1 Where is Gettysburg located?

2 The Battle of Gettysburg, which raged from July 1 to July 3, 1863, was the most lethal of the Civil War. How many lives were lost?

3 How was the battle of Gettysburg the most pivotal of the Civil War?

4 Under what circumstances was the Gettysburg Address delivered?

5 Who was the featured speaker?

Answers

1. In southeastern Pennsylvania, 130 miles southwest of Philadelphia.

2. More than 4,700 Confederates and 3,100 Union soldiers were killed in the clash at Gettysburg. Total casualties were 46,286.

3. On July 4, 1863, **ROBERT E. LEE** ordered his shattered army back to Virginia. The Confederacy was never again able to mount a large-scale attack against the North.

4. On November 19, 1863, a crowd of more than 15,000 gathered at the battle-field in Gettysburg to consecrate a new Civil War cemetery.

5. The featured speaker of the day was not **ABRAHAM LINCOLN** but **EDWARD EVERETT** (1794–1865), the nation's most celebrated orator, who declaimed for two hours. After Lincoln's remarks, Everett took Lincoln aside and said, "My speech will soon be forgotten; yours never will. How gladly would I exchange my hundred pages for your twenty lines!"

HEROES

★ ★ ★ ★

A hero is a person admired for his or her courage, nobility, exploits, or achievements and regarded as an ideal or model. Heroes often risk their lives and sometimes die for us. We couldn't do without them.

America seems to be good at making heroes when they're needed. We see them in our daily lives: the police officer, the firefighter, the soldier, and the crusader for a just cause. Sometimes they rise to astonishing heights when circumstances require it. We certainly witnessed extraordinary bravery and sacrifice on 9/11. Identify the heroes on the following pages.

John Glenn, the first American to orbit the Earth

1 He helped establish freedom of the press in the American colonies. He refused to reveal his sources for a story he published in his newspaper in 1733 criticizing the British governor of New York. To punish him, the British arrested and tried him in 1735 for criminal libel. Andrew Hamilton, a Philadelphia lawyer, came to defend him. Hamilton argued that publishing the truth could not be libelous. The handpicked judges ordered the jury to find him guilty, but the jurors refused and delivered a verdict of not guilty.

2 He was a Polish immigrant who lived and worked in New York City. The British arrested him as a spy in 1776. Pardoned, he was hired to work as an interpreter for the British with their German mercenary troops. He secretly encouraged soldiers to desert and helped prisoners escape. He was arrested again in 1778, tried, and sentenced to death. He escaped to Philadelphia, where he helped finance the Revolution, both by lending large sums of his own money to the fledgling country and by arranging loans from France.

3 He is often called the Father of the American Navy. He joined the Continental Navy and served as first lieutenant aboard the *Alfred,* the first naval ship bought by the Continental Congress. He later captained the *Bonhomme Richard.* He battled a larger and better-armed squadron of British ships. When the British demanded he surrender, he said, "I have not yet begun to fight," and went on to defeat them soundly.

4 She became a heroine at the Battle of Fort Washington in northern Manhattan on November 16, 1776. As many wives did, she followed her husband, John, while he served in the army, to cook for him, wash his clothes, and help tend the wounded. John and another soldier manned one of two cannons at Fort Washington. When the two men were killed, she took their place at the cannon. Seriously wounded and permanently disabled, she became the first woman in America to receive a military pension.

5 He was a Yale-educated teacher who became a captain in the

Continental Army and a member of a select group of fighters called the Rangers. He volunteered to go through the British lines to gather intelligence on troop positions in New York City. At the age of twenty-one, he was captured and hanged as a spy. Before he was hanged, he is credited with saying, "I regret that I have but one life to give for my country."

6 Famous as a hunter, Indian fighter, army scout, and teller of tall tales, he described himself as "fresh from the backwoods, half horse, half alligator, a little touched with the snapping turtle." He used his mythic reputation to build a political career, including elected service in the Tennessee legislature and the U.S. House of Representatives. His motto was, "Be always sure you're right—then go ahead!" He died at the Alamo fighting for Texas's independence from Mexico. After his passing, he continued to be the subject of songs, books, television programs, and movies.

7 He was one of America's most active abolitionists. He was publisher of the abolitionist newspaper the *Liberator*

and a founder of the American Anti-Slavery Society. He worked his whole life to end slavery and saw his goal realized at the end of the Civil War.

Hanged as a spy at age twenty-one

8 She led the early battle for women's suffrage and for the abolition of slavery. She and **LUCRETIA MOTT** (1793–1880) organized the 1848 Seneca Falls Convention, the nation's first public women's rights meeting. In 1865, she broke with the abolitionists, who favored the vote for African American men, but not for any women, black or white. In 1869, **SUSAN B. ANTHONY** (1820–1906) and she founded the National Woman Suffrage Association. She served as president of the association and its successor organization, the National American Woman Suffrage Association, for more than thirty years.

9 She started her career as a teacher and clerk, but became interested in the health field. During the Civil War, she cared for wounded soldiers on the battlefield. When the war ended, she created a bureau to look for missing men. On a trip to Switzerland, she learned about the Red Cross, based in Zurich. She worked with the organization during the Franco-Prussian War. In 1873, she returned to the United States to facilitate the creation of the American Red Cross. She was president of the organization from 1882 to 1904, when she retired.

10 He had to leave school after only three years. His family moved from Scotland to Allegheny, Pennsylvania, when he was fourteen, and arrived in America penniless. He started work as a messenger boy for a telegraph company and rose to become one of the richest men in America as the founder of a major steel company. In 1901, he sold his company for $480 million. He believed in philanthropy; over his remaining years, he gave away more than 90 percent of his fortune. As part of his charitable effort, he founded three thousand libraries and educated the people to staff them. He also funded the construction of seven thousand church organs.

11 Born into a wealthy abolitionist family, he was a white Union colonel who commanded the all-black 54th Massachusetts Infantry Regiment, which entered the Civil War in 1863. Depicted in the 1989 film *Glory,* he

perished in the Second Battle of Fort Wagner at the age of twenty-five.

12 He was a U.S. Army officer and civil engineer who supervised the construction and opening of the Panama Canal, completed two years ahead of schedule. The first ship traversed the canal on August 15, 1914. About one thousand ships and boats crossed the Isthmus of Panama that year. More than 13,660 crossed in 2013,

Founded the American Birth Control League

each taking between twenty and thirty hours. The American Society of Civil Engineers named the Panama Canal one of the seven wonders of the modern world.

13 She became blind and deaf at the age of nineteen months because of illness. Wild and unruly, she didn't learn to talk and had no way of communicating. Shortly before her seventh birthday, **ANNE SULLIVAN** (1866–1936), a remarkable teacher, came into her life. Anne taught her to sign and to read and write in Braille. By the time she was sixteen, she learned to speak. She graduated from Radcliffe College cum laude and became an author, speaker, political activist, recipient of the Presidential Medal of Freedom, and member of the National Institute of Arts and Letters. She traveled and lectured throughout the world, working to improve the lives of the blind and the deaf-blind.

14 She began her career as an obstetrical nurse in 1912 in New York City. In her work with the poor, she saw the problems created by unwanted pregnancies—poverty and high rates of infant and maternal deaths. She believed in the equality of women and men and believed that equality would not be realized until women had information about birth control. Although it was illegal in New York, in 1916, she opened a clinic to distribute birth control information and devices. She was arrested and sent to prison, and her legal appeals brought publicity to her cause. She later promoted the passage of a law allowing doctors to give birth control information to their patients. In 1921, she founded the American Birth Control League, which later became the Planned Parenthood Federation of America, and was also instrumental in founding the International Planned Parenthood Federation.

15 He was the leading U.S. air ace in World War I. Before that, he had been an internationally known race car driver, but in 1917 he joined the army. A pilot must shoot down five enemy aircraft to be counted as an ace. He shot down twenty-two planes and four balloons. In World War II, he served again, this time as a civilian inspector of air bases in the United States and overseas. In 1942, he was in a plane that was forced down in the Pacific. Along with six compatriots, he survived twenty-four days in a rubber raft before being rescued.

16 He made the first nonstop solo flight from New York to Paris on May 20 and 21, 1927, and won a $25,000 prize offered by a New York City hotel owner. Known as "Lucky Lindy" and the "Lone Eagle," he took off in the *Spirit of St. Louis* from Roosevelt Field in Garden City, Long Island. He flew 3,500 miles in thirty-three and one-half hours, supplied with only four sandwiches and two gallons of water. When he reached Le Bourget Field in Paris, ten thousand Parisians welcomed him. He was an instant hero

Flew nonstop across the Atlantic

worldwide. In the United States, he was so popular that a dance craze was called the Lindy Hop.

17 In 1962, this World War II and Korean War fighter pilot became the fifth man to travel in space and the first American to orbit the Earth. In 1998, after serving twenty-four years in the Senate, he, at age seventy-seven, lifted off for a second space flight thirty-six years after his first mission. His nine-day journey by the oldest-ever astronaut was designed to study the effects of space flight on the elderly.

18 He was awarded the Presidential Medal of Freedom posthumously in 1994 in recognition of his nonviolent activism and support of working people. A labor organizer, he started the National Farm Workers Association, which later became the United Farm Workers. He led strikes and successful nationwide boycotts of grapes and lettuce to win better working conditions for field workers. His birthday, March 31, has become a holiday in a growing number of states.

Answers

1. John Peter Zenger (1697–1746)
2. Haym Salomon (1740–1785)
3. John Paul Jones (1747–1792)
4. Margaret Cochran Corbin (1751–1800)
5. Nathan Hale (1755–1776)
6. Davy Crockett (1786–1836)
7. William Lloyd Garrison (1805–1879)
8. Elizabeth Cady Stanton (1815–1902)
9. Clara Barton (1821–1912)
10. Andrew Carnegie (1835–1919)
11. Robert Gould Shaw (1837–1863)
12. George Washington Goethals (1858–1928)
13. Helen Keller (1880–1968)
14. Margaret Sanger (1879–1966)
15. Eddie Rickenbacker (1890–1973)
16. Charles Lindbergh (1902–1974)
17. John Glenn (1921–)
18. César Chávez (1927–1993)

IMMORTAL MORTALS

ELBRIDGE GERRY (1744–1814), a vice president to James Madison, is the inspiration for a political term in our English language.

In 1812, in an effort to sustain his party's power, Gerry, who was then governor of Massachusetts, divided that state into electoral districts with more regard to politics than to geographical reality.

To a drawing of one of the governor's districts, Gilbert Stuart—the same fellow who had painted several famous portraits of George Washington—added a head, eyes, wings, and claws. According to one version of the story, Stuart exclaimed about his creation,

"That looks like a salamander!" "No," countered the editor of the newspaper in which the cartoon was to appear, "Better call it a Gerrymander!" The verb *gerrymander* is still used today to describe the shaping of electoral entities for political gain.

Thousands of common words in our language are born from proper names. These words often lose their reference to specific persons and become generic terms in our dictionaries; when they do, they usually shed their capital letters.

Here's a quiz in which you are asked to identify ten common words and the names of the immortalized Americans from whom they derive.

1 **SAMUEL AUGUSTUS** _____ (1803–1870), a San Antonio rancher, acquired vast tracts of land and dabbled in cattle raising. When he neglected to brand the calves born into his herd, his neighbors began calling the unmarked offspring by his name. Today this word has come to designate any nonconformist.

2 _____, the name of a courageous Apache warrior chief

Apache warrior chief

(1829–1909), became a battle cry for World War II paratroopers.

3 **AMELIA JENKS** _____ (1818–1894) was a feminist who helped to publicize the soon-to-be-fashionable puffy ladies' drawers that seemed to bloom like linen flowers.

4 A century before Elvis Presley, the handsome face of Union Army general **AMBROSE E.** _____ (1824–1881) was adorned by luxuriant side-whiskers sweeping down from his ears to his clean-shaven chin.

5 A colorful plant characterized by scarlet leaves is especially popular at Christmastime. This plant takes its name from **JOEL R.** _____ (1779–1851), our first ambassador to Mexico, who, in 1825, introduced it to the United States from its native land south of our border.

6 **SYLVESTER** _____ (1794–1851), a dietary reformer, donated the name of a cracker made of ground whole wheat flour to our language.

7 A children's nonalcoholic cocktail made from club soda, grenadine, and a maraschino cherry takes the name of _____ _____ (1928–2014), the most famous of all child movie stars.

8 In the heyday of the cowboy, **JOHN B.** _____ (1830–1906) created a hat with a high crown to hold a cushion of warm air and a wide brim to deflect rain and snow. A trapper offered him a five-dollar gold piece for the hat, and he sold it right off his head. He knew he had a winner.

9 _____ **STRAUSS** (1829–1902) was a German-Jewish immigrant who founded the first company to manufacture blue jeans. During the California gold rush days, he invented work trousers with copper rivets at the corners of the pockets so that the pants would not tear when loaded with samples of ore. The trousers continue to feature the now superfluous rivets, and young people go to extraordinary lengths to make a new pair look old and ratty.

10 For the 1893 Chicago World's Fair, **GEORGE WASHINGTON GALE** _____ (1859–1896) built a great wheel. It revolved on a stationary axle, stood 264 feet high, and carried thirty-six cars, each capable of seating sixty people. While few wheels that came after have matched the grandeur of the prototype, the attraction dominates almost every amusement park and carnival.

Answers

1. maverick—Maverick
2. Geronimo!—Geronimo
3. bloomers—Bloomer
4. sideburn—Burnside
5. poinsettia—Poinsett
6. graham cracker—Graham
7. Shirley Temple—Shirley Temple
8. Stetson—Stetson
9. Levi's—Levi
10. Ferris wheel—Ferris

INVENTORS

★ ★ ★ ★

Tinkering is a time-honored American pastime. Many men and women can't leave well enough alone. They're always trying to create something or improve something. As with most creative people, they benefit from the work of those who came before them, but they add that little spark of genius that can take their invention figuratively or literally into the stratosphere.

1 Which two American presidents got in on the act of inventing?

2 For what invention is **ELI WHITNEY** (1765–1825) famous?

3 **ROBERT FULTON** (1765–1815) tried several different careers, including fine art, before he settled on being an engineer and inventor. For which invention is he most famous?

4 Trained as an artist, **SAMUEL F. B. MORSE** (1791–1872) turned to invention as a career. It took him five years to achieve his first big success. What was it?

5 **ALEXANDER GRAHAM BELL (1847–1922), A TEACHER OF THE DEAF, CAME TO THE UNITED STATES FROM SCOTLAND IN 1871. WHAT MAJOR INVENTION DID HE PATENT IN 1876?**

6 What did Bell say the first time he used his invention?

7 Who was the Wizard of Menlo Park?

8 Name some of **THOMAS EDISON**'s inventions.

9 What were the first words that Thomas Edison spoke when testing his new tinfoil phonograph on December 6, 1877?

10 Who was **GEORGE WASHINGTON CARVER** (c. 1862–1943)?

Thomas Edison

11 Who invented modern air conditioning in 1902, and what was his initial goal?

12 Two wrongs don't make a right, but two Wrights did make an airplane. When and where?

13 In 1915, **CLARENCE BIRDSEYE** (1886–1956) went on a fur-trading and fishing trip to Labrador. To what invention did that trip lead?

14 **PHILO T. FARNSWORTH** (1906–1971) is credited with which invention?

George Washington Carver

15 **WHAT WAS THE VERY FIRST MESSAGE THAT ALEXANDER GRAHAM BELL HEARD DURING HIS FIRST PHONE CALL?**

16 Who was Alexander Graham Bellofsky?

17 What would you get if you crossed our first president with a wood sculptor?

18 Why was Thomas Edison exhausted after he invented the light bulb?

★　★　★　★

Answers

1. **THOMAS JEFFERSON** invented a collapsible writing table and a pedometer to measure his walks. **ABRAHAM LINCOLN** was the only president to be awarded a patent, for a system of buoying vessels over shoals.

2. In 1793, **ELI WHITNEY** invented the cotton gin (*gin* from "engine"), a machine that separated seeds from short-staple cotton fibers. This revolutionized cotton growing in the South, making it profitable. Previously one man, probably a slave, could clean one pound of cotton a day. A cotton gin could clean fifty pounds a day. Cotton became America's main export by 1850.

3. Fulton's greatest fame came from the *Clermont,* the first commercially successful steamboat. The *Clermont* made its first trip, from New York City up the Hudson River to Albany, on August 17, 1807, cutting the usual sailing time from sixty-four hours to thirty-two hours for the one-hundred-and-fifty-mile trip.

4. Morse invented the telegraph and created Morse code. In 1844, he built a test line between Baltimore and Washington, D.C., and tapped out the message "What hath God wrought!"—a sentence from biblical Numbers 23:23.

5. Bell patented the first telephone.

6. Bell's friend and colleague **THOMAS A. WATSON** answered Bell's first telephone call in 1876. Bell said, "Mister Watson, come here. I want you."

7. **THOMAS ALVA EDISON** (1847–1931), the world's most famous and prolific inventor, and one who followed his own motto: "Genius is 1 percent inspiration and 99 percent perspiration."

8. Edison's greatest invention may have been the Invention Factory. He created the first modern industrial research laboratory and worked ceaselessly to develop or improve many products. Edison invented the light bulb, the phonograph, the mimeograph, and the Dictaphone. He improved the telegraph, telephone, and motion picture projector. He held a record 1,093 U.S. patents and thousands of patents in other countries.

9. Thomas Edison read Sara Josepha Hale's "Mary Had a Little Lamb."

10. Born a slave, Carver recognized that cotton, the main crop of the South, was depleting the soil and that farmers needed profitable substitute crops. He developed 118 products from sweet potatoes and 300 from peanuts. By 1940, peanuts were the South's second largest cash crop, after cotton.

11. WILLIS CARRIER (1876–1950) tried to figure out how to reduce the humidity in a Brooklyn, New York, printing plant because of quality control problems when the humidity was high.

12. The **WRIGHT BROTHERS—WILBUR** (1867–1912) and **ORVILLE** (1871–1948)— became interested in flight when, in 1896, they read of the death of glider pioneer Otto Lilienthal. On December 17, 1903, Orville made the first controlled flight of a heavier-than-air machine near Kitty Hawk, North Carolina, a 120-foot trip that lasted all of twelve seconds. The top speed was seven miles per hour and top altitude 10 feet. Brother Wilbur ran alongside.

13. Watching the Inuit freeze fish and caribou meat, Birdseye noted that quickly frozen food was fresher, better textured, and more flavorful than food that had been slowly frozen. In 1925, Birdseye developed a process for flash freezing small packages of food. Frozen foods became popular in the 1950s, when freezers became widely available and TV dinners took over living rooms.

14. Farnsworth invented electronic television. On September 7, 1927, Farnsworth's image dissector camera sent the first visual, a simple straight line. Today, more than 99 percent of American homes have televisions, most more than one.

15. "Your call is important to us. Please continue to hold. Your call will be answered in the order it was received, and it may be monitored for quality assurance."

16. The first telephone Pole.

17. George Washington Carver.

18. Because he wasn't able to sleep with the light on.

MONUMENTS
AND
SYMBOLS

★ ★ ★ ★

Symbols are shorthand for complex and passionate ideas and experience. They have an importance beyond their physical existence. Sometimes they're created deliberately, as were the American flag or the Washington Monument. Other times they grow from their context and proximity to history, like the Liberty Bell.

1 In May 1776, a committee that included **GEORGE WASHINGTON** visited this upholsterer and asked her to create the first American flag. Who was she?

2 When did the symbol Uncle Sam begin life?

3 During the siege of the Revolutionary War capital of Philadelphia, what item that later became an iconic artifact was spirited out of the city?

4 What is the inscription that appears on the Liberty Bell?

5 **THOMAS NAST** (1840–1902), perhaps the most famous political cartoonist in our history, was responsible for the popularity of two party animals. Identify them.

6 What marble obelisk is the tallest stone structure in the world?

7 **WHY DOES THE WASHINGTON MONUMENT SLIGHTLY CHANGE COLOR ONE-THIRD OF THE WAY UP?**

8 Out of what material was the tip of the Washington Monument constructed?

9 The Statue of Liberty (Liberty Enlightening the World) was dedicated on October 28, 1886. What country gifted us with this national monument?

10 What is the source of the inspiring line "Give me your tired, your poor, your huddled masses yearning to breathe free"?

11 The Statue of Liberty's thin copper skin is supported by an iron framework constructed by the designer of another famous monument. Name him.

12 Identify the four presidents who are sculpted into Mount Rushmore.

13 Where is Mount Rushmore located, and who was the sculptor who carved the presidents into its rock?

14 What did one flag say to the other flag?

15 What did Betsy Ross do when she asked some colonists their opinion of the flag she had made?

16 What's red, white, black, and blue?

17 What's big, cracked, and carries your luggage?

18 How can we tell that the Statue of Liberty loves America?

Answers

1. BETSY ROSS (1752–1836), who suggested alterations to the original design, in particular changing the six-pointed stars to five-pointed because she could create each one with a single snip of her scissors. She continued to make American flags for another fifty years as part of her business.

2. Uncle Sam was first mentioned during the War of 1812. He is thought to have originated in a reference to one **SAMUEL WILSON**, who sold beef to the U.S. Army. **J. M. FLAGG** painted the most famous representation of Uncle Sam for the cover of *Leslie's Weekly* of July 6, 1916. The painting was used to create the famous recruiting poster, prominent in both world wars, that shows Uncle Sam pointing his finger at the viewer and insisting, "I Want You for U.S. Army."

3. Because bells could easily be recast into cannons, the bell that was later to be called the "Liberty Bell" and all the other bells in Philadelphia were hastily taken down from their towers on September 1777 and hidden. They were returned to Philadelphia in June 1778, after the British occupation ended.

4. The bell's inscription, "Proclaim liberty throughout all the land unto all the inhabitants thereof," echoes biblical Leviticus 25:10.

5. During the election of 1828, opponents of **PRESIDENT ANDREW JACKSON** labeled him a "jackass" for his populist beliefs. Jackson was entertained by the notion and ended up using it to his advantage on his campaign posters. Nast is credited with making Jackson's donkey the recognized symbol of the Democratic Party through one of his cartoons that appeared in *Harper's Weekly* in 1870. Four years later, also in *Harper's Weekly*, Nast drew a donkey clothed in lion's skin, scaring away all the animals at the zoo. One of those animals, the elephant, was labeled "The Republican Vote." That's all it took for the elephant to become associated with Republicans.

6. Towering a record 555 feet high, the Washington Monument honors **GEORGE WASHINGTON** and, for many, symbolizes the city of Washington, D.C.

Surrounded by fifty American flags, the monument stands near the center of the National Mall.

7. Marble from one quarry was used from 1848 until 1856 and, after a twenty-year hiatus, marble from another from 1876 to 1884, when the obelisk was finally dedicated.

8. The tip of the Washington Monument was constructed out of a material that, in 1884, was one of the rarest, most precious substances on Earth—aluminum.

9. Standing on Liberty Island in New York Harbor, Lady Liberty was a gift of friendship from the people of France to the people of the United States commemorating the alliance between the two nations during the Revolutionary War.

10. A bronze plaque inside the base of the Statue of Liberty displays the Emma Lazarus (1849–1887) poem "The New Colossus," written in 1883, which contains this eternally luminous line.

11. Lady Liberty's support was designed by **ALEXANDRE GUSTAVE EIFFEL** (1832–1923), the engineer who later designed the Eiffel Tower.

12. From left to right, the images of presidents **GEORGE WASHINGTON**, **THOMAS JEFFERSON**, **THEODORE ROOSEVELT**, and **ABRAHAM LINCOLN** appear on 5,725-foot-high Mount Rushmore.

13. Mount Rushmore is located in the Black Hills of South Dakota, twenty-three miles southwest of Rapid City. This national monument was created under the direction of sculptor **GUTZON BORGLUM** (1867–1941), who worked on the project from 1927 until his death. The heads are about 60 feet high.

14. Nothing. It just waved. 🙂

15. She invented the first flag poll. 🙂

16. Uncle Sam falling down the steps. 🙂

17. The Liberty Bell-hop. 🙂

18. She carries a torch for us. 🙂

NATIVE
AMERICANS

★ ★ ★ ★

As the apocryphal tale spins out, back in the early colonial days, a white hunter and a friendly Native American made a pact before they started out on the day's hunt. Whatever they bagged was to be divided equally between them.

At the end of the day, the white man undertook to distribute the spoils, consisting of several buzzards and turkeys. He suggested to his fellow hunter, "Either I take the turkeys and you the buzzards, or you take the buzzards and I take the turkeys." At this point the Native American complained, "You talk buzzard to me. Now talk turkey." And ever since, *to talk turkey* has meant "to tell it like it is." Let's talk turkey about our Native American heritage.

1 What were the populations of Europe and the Americas when Columbus first saw San Salvador (in the Bahamas) in 1492?

2 The Jamestown, Virginia, area was not vacant in 1607, when 105 English settlers led by John Smith established a colony there. Who were their neighbors?

3 Relations between the Indians and Jamestown colonists were rocky. What teenage woman aided the survival of Jamestown?

4 What happened to **POCAHONTAS** after she married **JOHN ROLFE**?

Pocahontas

5 Some English settlers in Massachusetts moved south to establish Connecticut in 1636. What happened when Pequot Indians resisted their incursions?

6 Many Native American groups in contact with the early settlers were farmers. What were their main crops?

7 Pronouncing many of the Native American words was difficult for the early explorers and settlers. In many instances, they had to shorten and simplify the names. Given the Native American names, identify the following animals: *apossoun, otchock, rahaugcum,* and *segankw.*

8 Who was **SACAGAWEA** (c. 1787–1812)?

9 Who was **TECUMSEH** (1768–1813)?

10 What future president struck a blow against Tecumseh's efforts to unite Indian nations against U.S. encroachment?

11 Enforcing the Indian Removal Act of 1830, **PRESIDENT ANDREW JACKSON** ordered Indian tribes in the South to move west of the Mississippi. What happened?

12 In the first half of the eighteenth century, mapmakers called the Great American Desert (the land west of the Mississippi) uninhabitable. Was it?

13 Native Americans were pushed out of their territories by farmers and cattlemen after the Civil War. What was the final blow to their resistance?

Tecumseh

14 The last major battle of the Indian Wars was fought on December 29, 1890. It still has political echoes today. Where did it take place?

15 Twenty-five of our fifty states trace their origins to Native American words. How many can you identify?

Two explorers with guide Sacagawea

Answers

1. Europe's population is estimated at 60 million, the Americas' from 40 to 100 million. Population in the Americas dropped 40–80 percent after the introduction of small pox, measles, influenza, and other diseases.

2. Algonquian Indians. **POWHATAN** (1545–1618), chief of the Powhatan Confederacy, ruled as many as 128 villages with 9,000 inhabitants along the James River.

3. **POCAHONTAS** (c. 1595–1617), daughter of Chief Powhatan, pleaded for the life of **CAPTAIN JOHN SMITH**, leader of the Jamestown colonists. Later, she married another colonist, **JOHN ROLFE**.

4. Pocahontas converted to Christianity. She, her husband, and son, Thomas, traveled to London, where she was presented at the court of **KING JAMES**. She died, possibly of smallpox, in England.

5. When relations between settlers and Indians deteriorated, men from Massachusetts and Connecticut, with their Narraganset Indian allies, massacred the Pequots. Those who survived were enslaved.

6. The Native Americans grew maize, peas, squash, pumpkins, and tobacco. They taught the colonists how to grow local plants.

7. The hidden animals are: *opossum* (Algonquian), *woodchuck* (Narraganset), *raccoon* (Algonquian), and *skunk* (Algonquian). To this menagerie we may add the likes of *caribou* (Micmac), *chipmunk* (Ojibwa), *moose* (Algonquian), and *muskrat* (Abenaki).

8. **SACAGAWEA** was a Shoshone Indian who, with her French-Canadian husband, **TOUSSAINT CHARBONNEAU**, accompanied Meriwether Lewis and William Clark as an interpreter. From Fort Mandan in what is now North Dakota, she walked thousands of miles with her infant son, Jean, on her back.

9. **TECUMSEH** was a Shawnee chief who in 1811 attempted to unite northern and southern Indians to defend their lands east of the Mississippi River.

10. On November 7, 1811, **WILLIAM HENRY HARRISON**, who was to become our ninth president (in 1841), defeated Native American followers of Tecumseh at the Battle of Tippecanoe in Indiana Territory.

11. Forced relocations started in 1831 with the Choctaw, and continued through 1832 with the Seminole, 1834 with the Creek, 1837 with the Chickasaw, and 1838 with the Cherokee. Thirty thousand Cherokee were forced onto the "Trail of Tears." One-quarter died before they reached their new "home" in Oklahoma. The South was now opened to more white settlers.

12. Two-thirds of the Indians west of the Mississippi lived in this "Great American Desert," now known as the Great Plains, including the Sioux, Blackfoot, Cheyenne, Crow, Arapaho, Pawnee, Kiowa, Apache, and Comanche. These migratory people depended on the buffalo for their living.

13. Railroads arrived and allowed products to be shipped east. The buffalo herds were systematically destroyed, first for hides, tallow, and meat; later for sport.

More than five million buffalo were killed in the early 1870s.

14. The massacre at Wounded Knee, South Dakota, occurred when troopers of the Seventh Cavalry surrounded a Lakota camp and tried to disarm the Indians. In less than an hour, between 150 and 300 Indian men, women, and children were killed.

15. Alabama, Alaska, Arkansas, Arizona, Connecticut, Idaho, Illinois, Iowa, Kansas, Kentucky, Massachusetts, Michigan, Minnesota, Mississippi, Missouri, Nebraska, North and South Dakota, Ohio, Oklahoma, Tennessee, Texas, Utah, Wisconsin, and Wyoming.

Indian village with tepees

PILGRIMS
AND
PURITANS

★ ★ ★ ★

I t's hard to imagine the lives of the people who thought that crossing an ocean in a tiny boat to an unknown land was better than staying where they were. For some it was the wrong choice, but others survived and flourished in their new home and started a new kind of country.

The first Thanksgiving

Pilgrims at Plymouth Rock

1 The Pilgrims established Plymouth Colony in 1620. The Puritans established Massachusetts Bay Colony in 1630. Who were the Pilgrims and the Puritans?

2 In 1620, the forty-one adult freemen aboard the *Mayflower* signed the Mayflower Compact. Why was it important?

3 Who was the first Pilgrim to step ashore at Plymouth Rock?

4 The Pilgrims first arrived at Cape Cod in late fall. How did they manage the winter?

5 What principles of law did the Puritans of the Massachusetts Bay Colony establish that have come down to us today?

6 Nonmembers of the Church of England sometimes left Massachusetts for Maryland. What attracted people there?

7 If April showers bring May flowers, what do May flowers bring? 😊

8 Why did the Pilgrims' pants always fall down? 😊

9 What was the Pilgrims' favorite kind of music? 😊

10 How are Puritans and small investors alike? 😊

The Mayflower

Answers

1. The Pilgrims and the Puritans were dissenters from the Church of England. The Pilgrims separated from the church, while the Puritans believed in reform from within.

2. The Mayflower Compact was an agreement to create "a civil body politic" to frame "just and equal laws." These were the first seeds of democracy.

3. The Pilgrims first sighted land on November 9, 1620. The first place they stepped ashore was at what would later be Provincetown. No one knows who the first ashore was there, or at Plymouth in December. It's not known that they stepped ashore at Plymouth Rock, either, although we celebrate that as the location. The Pilgrims never mentioned it. Additionally, they didn't call themselves "Pilgrims." That term didn't come into popular use until the 1790s.

4. Ill prepared, more than half died of hunger and disease, including scurvy. The survivors looted corn from an abandoned Indian village. The inhabitants had left or died in an epidemic—probably smallpox or leptospirosis imported by European ships. The epidemic had wiped out up to 90 percent of the Indians along the Massachusetts coast.

5. The Puritans established trial by jury, the protection of life and property by due process, and freedom from self-incrimination.

6. In England, Catholics had to attend Church of England services, contribute to the support of ministers, and make an oath to the king denying the pope's authority. **KING CHARLES I** granted a charter for Maryland to Roman Catholic **LORD BALTIMORE** in 1632. All Christians were welcome there. In 1649, Maryland passed the Toleration Act to allow religious freedom to all Christians.

7. Pilgrims. 🐢

8. Because they wore their buckles on their hats. 🐢

9. Plymouth Rock. 🐢

10. They have both been punished in stocks. 🐢

POETRY

★ ★ ★ ★

Poetry has been an integral part of American life from our beginning. Explorers sometimes included poetry in their reports. Native Americans wove poetry into their traditions. The first poetry published in America may have been that of **THOMAS MORTON** of Merrymount (now Quincy), Massachusetts, in 1627.

Let us not forget that **FRANCIS SCOTT KEY**'s "*Oh say, can you see, by the dawn's early light/What so proudly we hailed at the twilight's last gleaming?*" and **KATHERINE LEE BATES**'s "*America! America!/God shed his grace on thee/And crown thy good with brotherhood/From sea to shining sea!*" were first written as poems and only afterward set to music.

What follows are some of the most memorable and enduring lines in the mighty line of American poetry. Identify the sources of each quotation by title and author.

Known for his poem "The Song of Hiawatha"

1

*Once upon a midnight dreary,
    while I pondered, weak and weary,
Over many a quaint and curious volume
    of forgotten lore—*

2

*By the shores of Gitche Gumee
By the shining Big-Sea-Water*

3

*The outlook wasn't brilliant
    for the Mudville nine that day;
The score stood four to two,
    with but one inning more to play.*

4

*Because I could not stop for Death,
He kindly stopped for me—*

5

*Behind him lay the gray Azores,
Behind the Gates of Hercules;
Before him not the ghost of shores,
Before him only shoreless seas.*

Known for his poem "The Raven"

6

*The fog comes
On little cat feet.*

7

*All I could see from where I stood
Was three long mountains and a wood.*

8

The woods are lovely, dark and deep,
But I have promises to keep,
And miles to go before I sleep,
And miles to go before I sleep.

9

This is the way the world ends
Not with a bang but a whimper.

10

What happens to a dream deferred?
Does it dry up like a raisin in the sun?

Known for
her poem
"Renascence"

Answers

1. "The Raven" (1845), **EDGAR ALLAN POE** (1809–1849)
2. "The Song of Hiawatha" (1855), **HENRY WADSWORTH LONGFELLOW** (1807–1882)
3. "Casey at the Bat" (1888), **ERNEST LAWRENCE THAYER** (1863–1940)
4. "Because I could not stop for Death" (1890), **EMILY DICKINSON** (1830–1886)
5. "Columbus" (1892), **JOAQUIN MILLER** (1837–1913)
6. "Fog" (1916), **CARL SANDBURG** (1878–1967)
7. "Renascence" (1912), **EDNA ST. VINCENT MILLAY** (1892–1950)
8. "Stopping by Woods on a Snowy Evening" (1922), **ROBERT FROST** (1874–1963)
9. "The Hollow Men" (1925), **T. S. ELIOT** (1888–1965)
10. "Dream Deferred" (1951), **LANGSTON HUGHES** (1902–1967)

PRESIDENTIAL
FIRSTS

★ ★ ★ ★

When George Washington became our first president in 1789, other national leaders included the king of France, the czarina of Russia, the emperor of China, and the shogun of Japan. Today, no king rules France, no czar rules Russia, no emperor rules China, and no shogun rules Japan, but the office of president of the United States endures.

Our first president, George Washington

1 Who was the first vice president to become president?

2 Who was the first president born a United States citizen?

3 Who was the first president to campaign actively?

4 Who was the first vice president to assume the presidency because of the death of the president?

5 Who was the first president to be photographed while in office?

William Henry Harrison

6 Who was the first president to serve under a name other than his birth name?

7 Who was the first president to establish a national park?

8 Who was the first president to ride in an automobile?

9 Who was the first president to fly in an airplane?

10 Who was the first president to travel abroad during his term?

John Adams

John F. Kennedy

11 Who was the first president to win a Nobel Prize?

12 Who was the first president in whose election women were allowed to vote?

13 Who was the first president born west of the Mississippi River?

14 Who was the first president to appoint a woman to his cabinet?

15 Which president started the tradition of the presidential library?

16 Who was the first president to have served in the U.S. Navy?

17 Who was the first president to name an African American to his cabinet?

18 Who was the first president to visit all fifty states, the Soviet Union, and China?

19 Who was the first president for whom eighteen-year-olds could vote?

20 Who was the first president to be impeached?

21 Who was the first president born in a hospital?

22 WHO WAS THE FIRST BABY BOOMER TO BE ELECTED PRESIDENT?

Answers

1. Vice President **JOHN ADAMS** succeeded George Washington as president in 1797. A total of fourteen vice presidents out of forty-seven have gone on to become president.

Martin Van Buren

2. MARTIN VAN BUREN, our eighth president, was born on December 5, 1782, making him the first president born after the Declaration of Independence was signed. Eight presidents were born before 1776 in the American colonies as British subjects—George Washington (1732), John Adams (1735), Thomas Jefferson (1743), James Madison (1751), James Monroe (1758), John Quincy Adams (1767), Andrew Jackson (1767), and William Henry Harrison (1773).

3. WILLIAM HENRY HARRISON was, in 1840, the first candidate to stump personally. His was the first campaign slogan: "Tippecanoe and Tyler, Too." The slogan referred to Harrison's nickname, which he acquired after his victory in 1811 at the Battle of Tippecanoe. He defeated a group of Shawnee Indian followers of Tecumseh, who were organizing to oppose white incursions into Indian territory. "Tyler" refers to his running mate, John Tyler (later our tenth president).

4. JOHN TYLER was the first vice president to be elevated to the presidency as a result of the death of the president, in this instance **WILLIAM HENRY HARRISON**, our ninth president, who died of pneumonia in 1841 after thirty-one days in office.

5. WILLIAM HENRY HARRISON was the first president to be photographed while in office. A daguerreotype, since lost, was made at his inauguration, on March 4, 1841. John Quincy Adams (sixth president), Andrew Jackson (seventh), and Martin Van Buren (eighth) were all photographed after serving their terms.

6. ULYSSES S. GRANT came into this world as Hiram Ulysses Grant. When his name was mistakenly entered on the West Point register as *Ulysses S. Grant,* he eagerly embraced the error because he detested the initials *H.U.G.* and loved having the initials *U.S.,* as in "United States" and "Uncle Sam." The *S.* stood for *Simpson,* his mother's maiden name. Two other presidents had their names legally changed. Leslie Lynch King Jr. became Gerald Rudolph Ford, and William Jefferson Blythe IV became William Jefferson Clinton. Both adopted the names of their stepfathers.

7. ULYSSES S. GRANT established Yellowstone as the nation's first national park on March 1, 1872. In 1936, **GERALD FORD** served as a park ranger in Yellowstone, the only president to have been employed by the National Park Service.

8. WILLIAM McKINLEY. In 1901, after our twenty-fifth president was shot, he was carried by an electric-powered ambulance to the hospital at the Pan-American Exposition. **WILLIAM HOWARD TAFT** was the first president to own an automobile. He had the White House stables converted to a four-car garage, which housed, among other vehicles, Baker Electric cars. That's right, some of the first automobiles in America were electric.

9. THEODORE ROOSEVELT was the first president to fly in an airplane. On October 11, 1910, a year and a half after he completed his terms in office, he took a four-minute flight in a biplane built by the Wright Brothers. The next Roosevelt—**FRANKLIN D. ROOSEVELT**—was the first president to ride in an airplane on official business. He flew in a Boeing 314 Flying Boat named the *Dixie Clipper* to a World War II strategy meeting with British Prime Minister Winston Churchill in Casablanca, Morocco, on January 14, 1943. He was also the first to have a presidential aircraft. The *Sacred Cow* was a C-54 Skymaster converted for presidential use. Roosevelt first traveled in it to the

Yalta Conference in February 1945, shortly before his death on April 12.

10. THEODORE ROOSEVELT was the first president to leave the United States while in office when he visited Panama in 1906. He was also the first president to visit each of the forty-six states that existed at the time. The first U.S. president to visit a European country while serving as president was **WOODROW WILSON**, who arrived at Brest, France, on December 13, 1918.

11. THEODORE ROOSEVELT won the Nobel Peace Prize in 1906 for mediating the Treaty of Portsmouth, which ended the Russo-Japanese War. **WOODROW WILSON** (1919), **JIMMY CARTER** (2002), and **BARACK OBAMA** (2009) were also accorded that honor.

12. WARREN G. HARDING won a smashing 60 percent of the popular vote, helped by women voting for the first time. He was a strong supporter in the Senate of the Nineteenth Amendment to the Constitution, which granted the vote to women. It was ratified in August 1920, just before the election.

13. HERBERT HOOVER was born in the village of West Branch, Iowa, in 1874, the first of only eight presidents born west of the Mississippi. The others are Harry S. Truman (1884), Lamar, Missouri; Dwight Eisenhower (1890), Denison, Texas; Lyndon Johnson (1908), Stonewall, Texas; Richard Nixon (1913), Yorba Linda, California; Gerald Ford (1913), Omaha, Nebraska; Bill Clinton (1946), Hope, Arkansas; and Barack Obama (1961), Honolulu, Hawaii.

14. FRANKLIN D. ROOSEVELT appointed the first woman—**FRANCES PERKINS**—to the cabinet in 1933. She remained secretary of labor until 1945.

15. FRANKLIN D. ROOSEVELT started the presidential library tradition in 1939, when he donated his papers to the United States and asked the National Archives to administer them. His presidential library in Hyde Park, New York, was dedicated in 1941.

16. If the army was the most common branch of military service for earlier presidents, the navy attracted the greatest number of presidents who served in the second half of the twentieth century. **JOHN F. KENNEDY** was the first president to have served in the U.S. Navy (1941–1945), followed by Lyndon Johnson (1941–1942), Richard Nixon (1942–1946), Gerald Ford (1942–1946), Jimmy Carter (1943–1953), and George H. W. Bush (1942–1945). A total of thirty-one presidents served in the military. Besides the U.S. Army and Navy, the others served in the Continental army and in various state militias.

17. LYNDON JOHNSON was the first president to appoint an African American to a cabinet post when, in 1966, he chose **ROBERT WEAVER** to head the new Department of Housing and Urban Development.

18. RICHARD NIXON was the first president to visit the Soviet Union (in 1972). He had previously visited there as vice president in 1959. He also visited China in 1972 and was the first president to visit all fifty states.

19. The Twenty-sixth Amendment to the Constitution, ratified by a majority of the states in 1971, during Richard Nixon's first term, granted suffrage to eighteen-year-olds.

20. If you answered Richard Nixon, you're mistaken. President Nixon resigned before any impeachment trial. **ANDREW JOHNSON** (1808–1875) on February 24, 1868, and **BILL CLINTON** on December 19, 1998, were tried under the articles of impeachment. Both were acquitted (Johnson by a single vote in the Senate).

21. Born on October 1, 1924 in Plains, Georgia, **JIMMY CARTER**, our thirty-ninth president, was the first president born in a hospital. Our only other presidents born in hospitals are **BILL CLINTON**, **GEORGE W. BUSH**, and **BARACK OBAMA**. All others were born at home.

22. Born after World War II on August 19, 1946, **BILL CLINTON** was the first baby boomer to be elected president. Born July 6, 1946, **GEORGE W. BUSH** was the second presidential boomer.

PRESIDENTIAL
MOSTS

★ ★ ★ ★

Who is the youngest man ever to have served as president of the United States? If your answer is John Fitzgerald Kennedy, you're not quite correct. Kennedy was, at the age of forty-three, the youngest man ever to have been *elected* president, but **THEODORE ROOSEVELT** became president at forty-two, when William McKinley was assassinated.

Following is a gallery of other presidential record setters.

1 NOW THAT YOU KNOW WHO OUR YOUNGEST PRESIDENT WAS, WHO WAS OUR OLDEST PRESIDENT?

2 Which president lived the longest?

3 Which man spent the greatest number of years as a former president?

4 Which president spent the shortest period as a former president?

5 Which president lived the shortest?

6 Who was our tallest president?

7 Who was our shortest president?

8 Who was our fattest president?

9 Who was president for the shortest period of time?

10 Who was president for the longest period of time?

11 Which president had the greatest number of children?

12 Which president ran in the greatest number of presidential and vice presidential elections as a Republican?

13 Which president ran in the greatest number of presidential and vice presidential elections as a Democrat?

14 Who was our most traveled president?

Our tallest president

15 WHICH PRESIDENT WON THE LARGEST PERCENTAGE OF THE POPULAR VOTE SINCE THAT FIGURE BEGAN TO BE TABULATED IN 1824?

16 Who was our most athletic president?

17 How do we know that anyone can be elected president? 🐛

Ronald Reagan

Answers

1. The average age at which America's presidents have taken office is fifty-four. **RONALD REAGAN** became president at sixty-nine years and eleven months, older than anyone else, and left at seventy-seven years and eleven months. Before Reagan, **DWIGHT EISENHOWER** had been the only president to reach the age of seventy while in office.

2. When **RONALD REAGAN** died at the age of ninety-three years and 120 days, he was our longest-lived president. But, on November 12, 2006, **GERALD FORD** surpassed that record and lived another month and a half. Amazingly, our third longest-lived president is **JOHN ADAMS**, who was born in 1735 and who lived for ninety years and eight months, followed by **HERBERT HOOVER**, ninety years and two months.

3. In 2012, **JIMMY CARTER** surpassed Herbert Hoover's previous record of thirty-one years, seven months, and seventeen days as an ex-president.

James Polk

4. JAMES POLK proclaimed, "No president who performs his duties faithfully and conscientiously can have any leisure." He meant it: During Polk's four years in office, his wife, Sarah, and he spent only six weeks away from the job. During his term, no dancing, singing, or alcohol was permitted in the White House. He died just three months into his retirement, quite possibly from exhaustion.

5. JOHN F. KENNEDY took office at the age of forty-three, and after two and a half years was assassinated at the age of forty-six. **JAMES POLK** was our shortest-lived president to die out of office, at age fifty-three.

6. ABRAHAM LINCOLN, at 6 feet 4 inches, was our loftiest president. To the inevitable question "How tall are you?" Lincoln would reply, "Tall enough to reach the ground." **LYNDON JOHNSON** reached the second-greatest height at 6 feet 3 1/2 inches. **GEORGE WASHINGTON** and **THOMAS JEFFERSON** measured up in third place at 6 feet 2 1/2 inches. Almost all our presidents have been taller than the average American living contemporaneously, and two-thirds of them have been taller than their closest opponent.

7. JAMES MADISON, at 5 feet 4 inches and weighing about a hundred pounds, was our most compact president. Madison may be our only president who weighed less than his IQ.

8. WILLIAM HOWARD TAFT, at 5 feet 11 1/2 inches and 335 to 340 pounds, was our fullest-figured president. After he left office, he dropped eighty pounds and kept it off until his death seventeen years later.

9. WILLIAM HENRY HARRISON died on the thirty-first day of his presidency. As a result, 1841 was a year in which three presidents served—Martin Van Buren, Harrison, and John Tyler.

10. FRANKLIN D. ROOSEVELT was elected to four terms as president and served from 1933 to 1945. This record can't be broken as long as the Twenty-second Amendment, ratified in 1951 and setting a limit of two terms, remains in effect. The exact wording is: "No person shall be elected to the office of the President more than twice, and no person who has held the office of President, or acted as President, for more than two years of a term to which some other person was elected President shall be elected to the office of the President more than once."

11. JOHN TYLER was the most fatherly of presidents. He had three sons and five daughters with his first wife, Letitia, and five sons and two daughters with his second, Julia, for a total of fifteen offspring. From a single marriage, to his wife, Anna, **WILLIAM HENRY HARRISON** was the father of ten children—four girls and six boys, one of whom became the father of another president, **BENJAMIN HARRISON**. Hence, the Harrison-Tyler ticket of 1840 was by far the most prolific in American history—engendering a total of twenty-five children!

12. RICHARD M. NIXON ran successfully as a Republican candidate for the office of vice president in 1952 and 1956, unsuccessfully for president in 1960, and successfully for president in 1968 and 1972. Total: five.

Franklin D. Roosevelt

13. FRANKLIN D. ROOSEVELT ran unsuccessfully as a Democratic candidate for the office of vice president in 1920 and successfully for president in 1932, 1936, 1940, and 1944. Total: five.

14. BILL CLINTON set a record for the most trips abroad during a presidency: 133.

15. In 1964, **LYNDON B. JOHNSON** defeated Barry Goldwater by a margin of sixteen million votes and with 61.1 percent of the popular vote, the largest percentage ever recorded. **FRANKLIN ROOSEVELT**'s 523–8 Electoral College victory over Alfred M. Landon in 1936 was the largest electoral landslide since **JAMES MONROE** won all but a single Electoral College vote in 1820. In 1984, **RONALD REAGAN** received the greatest number of electoral votes—525. Loser Walter Mondale won only thirteen electoral votes (ten from his home state of Minnesota and three from the District of Columbia).

16. This is, of course, a matter of opinion, but we nominate **GERALD FORD**, who was a star center on the University

Gerald Ford

of Michigan football team. Ford turned down offers to play professionally for the Chicago Bears and the Green Bay Packers. He was head boxing coach and assistant football coach at Yale University. He was an above-average tennis player, and he scored a hole in one in the Memphis Golf Classic.

17. Jefferson did it, Nixon did it, and Truman did it, so obviously any Tom, Dick, and Harry can be elected president. 🐵

★ ★ ★ ★

PRESIDENTIAL ONLYS

W ho was the only president to run as the candidate of a major party in a presidential election and come in third?

In 1912, **PRESIDENT WILLIAM HOWARD TAFT** ran as a Republican for reelection against the Democratic nominee, **WOODROW WILSON**. Former president **THEODORE ROOSEVELT** also entered the presidential fray, as a candidate for the Bull Moose Party. Roosevelt and Taft split the Republican vote, and Wilson won handily. Taft placed third with an abysmal 23 percent of the popular vote, the lowest ever for an incumbent president. Unremittingly good humored, Taft sighed, "I have one consolation. No one candidate was ever elected ex-president by such a large majority."

Try your hand and brain at the following quiz about presidential onlys.

1 WHO WAS THE ONLY PRESIDENT WHO DID NOT REPRESENT A POLITICAL PARTY WHEN HE WAS FIRST ELECTED?

2 Who was the only president to be defeated by his vice president?

3 Who was the only president to found a university?

4 Who was the only president to have served in two different cabinet posts?

5 Who was the only president to serve in the House of Representatives after his presidency?

6 Who was the only president to have served in both the Revolution and the War of 1812?

7 Who was the only president for whom English was a second language?

Zachary Taylor

8 Who were the only two presidents who died in the White House?

9 Who was the only U.S. president to give up his U.S. citizenship?

10 Who was the only president to be the father-in-law of another president?

11 Who was the only president never to marry?

12 Who was the only president to serve in the Senate after his presidency?

13 Who was the only president to serve two nonconsecutive terms?

14 Who was the only president to serve as Supreme Court justice after his presidency?

15 Who were our only Quaker presidents?

16 Who was the only president with military service in both world wars?

17 Who was the only Roman Catholic president?

18 Who was the only president to resign from office?

19 Who was the only man to be vice president and president without being elected to either office?

20 Who was the only president to graduate from the U.S. Naval Academy?

21 Who was the only president to have been divorced?

22 Who was the only president to have headed a labor union?

23 Who was the only president to have been director of the Central Intelligence Agency?

24 Who was the only president to have been a Rhodes Scholar?

25 Who was the only Democratic president to win reelection during the second half of the twentieth century?

26 WHO WAS THE ONLY PRESIDENT TO HAVE EARNED AN MBA (MASTER OF BUSINESS ADMINISTRATION)?

Answers

1. Political parties didn't exist in America when **GEORGE WASHINGTON** was elected to his first term in 1788. They came into existence when **ALEXANDER HAMILTON** organized the Federalist Party in the early 1790s and **THOMAS JEFFERSON** opposed him with the Democratic-Republicans. In his farewell address, Washington warned about the danger of political parties leading to temporary or permanent despotism.

2. **JOHN ADAMS** was defeated in 1801 by his vice president, **THOMAS JEFFERSON**, the only president to experience that turnabout.

3. **THOMAS JEFFERSON** founded the University of Virginia in Charlottesville in 1819. Before they became U.S. presidents, **JAMES GARFIELD** was principal of Hiram College, **WOODROW WILSON** was president of Princeton University, and **DWIGHT EISENHOWER** president of Columbia University.

4. **JAMES MONROE** served as secretary of state and secretary of war, the only president to do so. His tenure in those jobs was during the War of 1812, in the administration of **JAMES MADISON**, the president who preceded him.

5. **JOHN QUINCY ADAMS** served in the House of Representatives for seventeen years and remains the only president to serve in the House after his presidential term ended. In 1848, he suffered a fatal stroke and fell to the floor of the House of Representatives. Missouri Senator Thomas Hart Benton eulogized, "Where else could death have found him but at the post of duty?"

6. **ANDREW JACKSON** was the only president to serve in both the Revolutionary War and the War of 1812. He was also the only president to have been a prisoner of war, captured during the Revolution at the age of thirteen, when he served as a courier. In the War of 1812, he earned his nickname, "Old Hickory." He also fought in the Creek War (1813–1814) and the First Seminole War (1814–1819).

7. **MARTIN VAN BUREN** was the first president of Dutch ancestry. He grew up speaking Dutch, and his wife, Hannah, and he spoke Dutch at home.

Herbert Hoover

himself as a citizen of the Confederate States of America. He died on January 18, 1862, in Virginia. His coffin was draped with a Confederate flag.

10. ZACHARY TAYLOR was the father-in-law of **JEFFERSON DAVIS**, president of the Confederacy. Three months after eloping with Davis, Taylor's daughter, twenty-one-year-old Sarah (1814–1835), died of malaria. Taylor bitterly blamed Davis for taking Sarah to malaria country, Louisiana, in the summer.

11. JAMES BUCHANAN was known as the Bachelor President. There's no clear proof, but during his life, many people thought Buchanan was homosexual.

8. Only two presidents died in the White House itself—**WILLIAM HENRY HARRISON** in 1841 and **ZACHARY TAYLOR** in 1850.

9. JOHN TYLER joined the Confederacy twenty years after he left office. He became the only U.S. president who did not consider himself a U.S. citizen. Although the United States never recognized the legitimacy of the Confederacy as a separate country, he thought of

12. ANDREW JOHNSON was the only former president elected to the U.S. Senate, the very body that almost kicked him out of office. His triumphant return to that body was short lived. In less than four months, he died of a stroke.

13. GROVER CLEVELAND was both our twenty-second and twenty-fourth president, forever confusing the mathematics of the presidential sequence.

14. When **WILLIAM HOWARD TAFT** was appointed chief justice of the Supreme Court eight years after his presidency, he became the only man ever to have headed both the executive and judicial branches of our government.

15. HERBERT HOOVER and **RICHARD NIXON** are our only presidents who were Quakers. They were eighth cousins once removed.

16. DWIGHT EISENHOWER served in World Wars I and II, and was the only general to be elected president in the twentieth century. Eleven other presidents had previously been generals: **GEORGE WASHINGTON, ANDREW JACKSON, WILLIAM HENRY HARRISON, ZACHARY TAYLOR, FRANKLIN PIERCE, ANDREW JOHNSON, ULYSSES S. GRANT, RUTHERFORD B. HAYES, JAMES GARFIELD, CHESTER A. ARTHUR**, and **BENJAMIN HARRISON**. At the other end of the ranks, **JAMES BUCHANAN** and **ABRAHAM LINCOLN** never rose above private. Twelve presidents had no military experience.

17. JOHN F. KENNEDY was the only Roman Catholic president. An earlier Catholic

Dwight Eisenhower

nominee for president, Al Smith, was soundly defeated by Herbert Hoover in 1928.

18. RICHARD NIXON resigned from the presidency on August 9, 1974, the only president to do so. **SPIRO AGNEW**, his first vice president, had resigned in 1973.

19. As a result of the events above, **GERALD FORD** was the only man who served as both vice president (replacing Agnew) and president (replacing Nixon) without having been elected to either office. The only elected office he ever held was a western Michigan congressional seat. Ford's vice president, **NELSON ROCKEFELLER**, was also never elected to his office.

20. The only president to have graduated from the U.S. Naval Academy was **JIMMY CARTER**, in the class of 1946. **ULYSSES S. GRANT** and **DWIGHT EISENHOWER** were the only presidents to have graduated from the U.S. Military Academy at West Point.

21. RONALD REAGAN was our only divorced president. A popular screen actor, he had been married to actress Jane Wyman. Actress Nancy Davis was his second and last wife.

22. RONALD REAGAN was president of the Screen Actors Guild.

23. GEORGE H. W. BUSH was the only president to have been director of the CIA.

24. BILL CLINTON graduated from Georgetown University, and in 1968 won a Rhodes Scholarship to Oxford University, the only president to have achieved that distinction.

25. In 1996, **BILL CLINTON** became the only Democratic president since **FRANKLIN D. ROOSEVELT** to win reelection, a span of more than fifty years.

26. GEORGE W. BUSH earned an MBA from the Harvard Business School, the only president to hold that degree. He went on to become managing general partner of the Texas Rangers baseball team.

George W. Bush

PRESIDENTIAL
QUOTES

★ ★ ★ ★

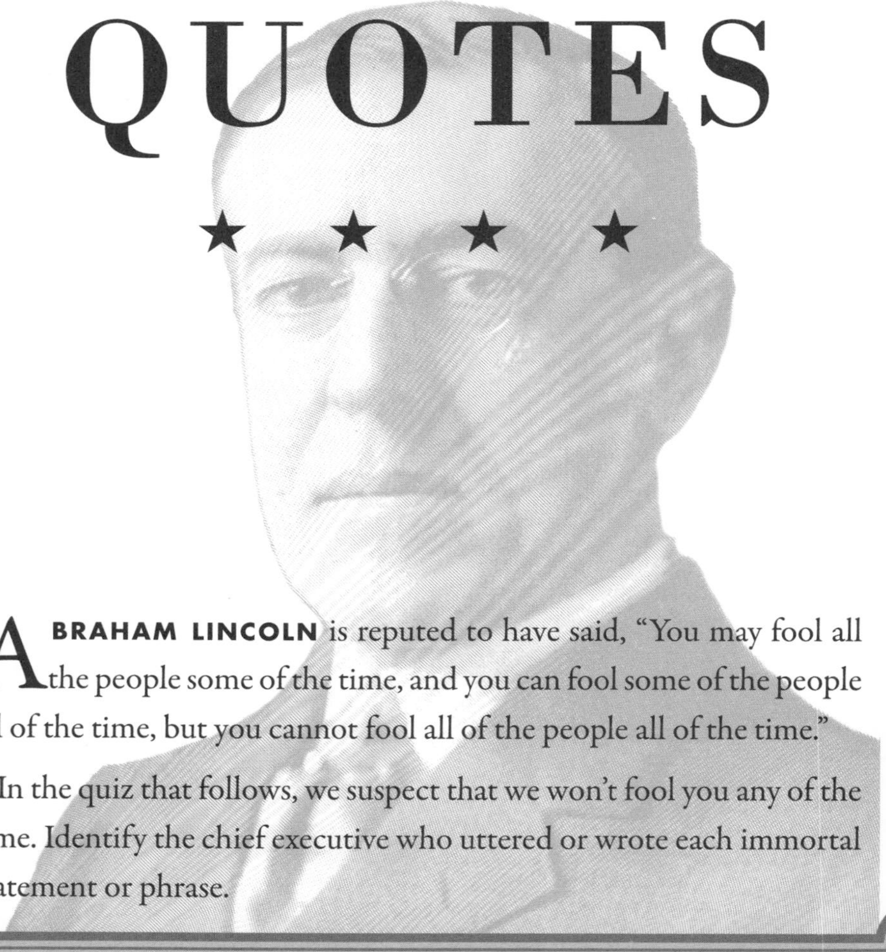

A BRAHAM LINCOLN is reputed to have said, "You may fool all the people some of the time, and you can fool some of the people all of the time, but you cannot fool all of the people all of the time."

In the quiz that follows, we suspect that we won't fool you any of the time. Identify the chief executive who uttered or wrote each immortal statement or phrase.

Woodrow Wilson

1 "WE HOLD THESE TRUTHS TO BE SELF-EVIDENT: THAT ALL MEN ARE CREATED EQUAL."

2 "The presidency is not a bed of roses."

3 "... that government of the people, by the people, and for the people shall not perish from the earth."

4 "Speak softly and carry a big stick."

5 "The world must be made safe for democracy."

6 "The business of America is business."

Calvin Coolidge

7 "... a chicken in every pot and a car in every garage."

8 "The only thing we have to fear is fear itself."

9 "The buck stops here."

10 "We must guard against the unwarranted influence, whether sought or unsought, by the military-industrial complex."

11 "Ask not what your country can do for you—ask what you can do for your country."

12 "I am not a crook."

13 "Our long national nightmare is over."

Harry S. Truman

14 "Government is not the solution to our problem. Government is the problem."

15 "... a thousand points of light ..."

16 "There is nothing wrong with America that cannot be cured by what is right with America."

Bill Clinton

Richard Nixon

Answers

1. Thomas Jefferson
2. James Polk
3. Abraham Lincoln
4. Theodore Roosevelt
5. Woodrow Wilson
6. Calvin Coolidge
7. Herbert Hoover
8. Franklin Roosevelt
9. Harry Truman
10. Dwight Eisenhower
11. John F. Kennedy
12. Richard Nixon
13. Gerald Ford
14. Ronald Reagan
15. George H. W. Bush
16. Bill Clinton

THE
REVOLUTIONARY
WAR

★ ★ ★ ★

The Revolution began on April 19, 1775. George Washington declared a cessation of hostilities on April 19, 1783. After exactly eight years and more than four thousand American battle deaths, America became the land of the free and the home of the brave.

1 Name the British monarch whom the American colonists defied because they were being taxed without being represented in Parliament.

2 American colonists were divided in their ties to the British crown. What were the names for those who remained loyal and those who yearned for independence?

3 What was the Stamp Act, passed by the British Parliament in 1765, and what was its result?

4 What pattern did widespread protests to the Stamp Act of 1765 establish?

5 What happened on March 5, 1770, outside the Boston Custom House?

6 **WHAT FUTURE PRESIDENT ACTED AS DEFENSE ATTORNEY FOR THE BRITISH TROOPS ON TRIAL FOR THE BOSTON MASSACRE OF 1770?**

7 In May 1773, Parliament passed the Tea Act to bail out the British East India Company. What was the act's most dramatic result?

8 What were the main results of the throwing of tea overboard at the Boston Tea Party on December 16, 1773?

9 Who said, "Give me liberty or give me death," and under what circumstances did he say it?

10 With what battles did the Revolutionary War begin?

11 Who coined the phrase "the shot heard 'round the world," and to what incident does it refer?

12 What famous poem begins: *"Listen, my children, and you shall hear/Of the midnight ride of Paul Revere"?*

13 Where did **PAUL REVERE**'s ride begin and end?

14 Who were the minutemen, and why were they so called?

15 On May 10, 1775, what contingent of American patriots captured the British-held garrison at Fort Ticonderoga?

16 On June 14, 1775, the Second Continental Congress appointed **GEORGE WASHINGTON** to what position?

17 What, where, and when was the Battle of Bunker Hill?

18 The American fighters lost the Battle of Bunker Hill, but from that bloody clash learned what significant lesson?

19 It's called "the most incendiary and popular pamphlet of the entire revolutionary era." Name the pamphlet and its author.

20 During the bleak winter of 1777–1778, where were George Washington and his forces encamped?

21 IDENTIFY THE AMERICAN GENERAL IN THE REVOLUTIONARY WAR WHOSE NAME HAS BECOME A BYWORD FOR TREASON.

22 What role did **MARIE-JOSEPH PAUL YVES ROCH GILBERT DU MOTIER, MARQUIS DE LAFAYETTE** (1757–1834) play in the Revolutionary War?

23 On December 23, 1783, **GENERAL GEORGE WASHINGTON** resigned his commission as commander-in-chief of the Continental army. What is the significance of that event?

24 UNESCO has designated twenty-one sites in the United States as World Heritage Sites, including which two associated with the Revolutionary War?

25 What happened as a result of the Stamp Act? 😊

26 What did the colonists wear at the Boston Tea Party? 😊

27 What did King George think of the American colonists? 😊

28 What did the colonists call the barnyard fowl they trained to capture British spies? 😊

29 What do you call a bunch of cattle gathered in a space satellite? 😊

30 Which one of George Washington's officers had the best sense of humor? 😊

31 What has four legs, a shiny nose, and fought for England? 😊

Regulators capturing a powder escort

Answers

1. KING GEORGE III, who reigned from 1760 to his death in 1820.

2. The loyalists were called Tories and those who wished to break from England were called Whigs. Those names originated with British political parties.

3. The Stamp Act was passed in 1765. Britain required the colonies to pay taxes on all paper preprinted in England, such as ship's papers, legal documents, licenses, books and newspapers, and even playing cards. Mass protests against such taxation without representation resulted, and the act was repealed in 1766.

4. During the street demonstrations against the Stamp Act, locally organized street groups began to coalesce into a new intercolonial network, a pattern for future resistance to the British that would propel America toward 1776.

5. On that snowy day occurred the Boston Massacre. British soldiers fired upon a crowd of American civilians, killing five and wounding six others.

6. JOHN ADAMS, who would become our second president, defended eight British soldiers accused of murder. Six were acquitted, and two, found guilty of manslaughter, received a branding on the hand.

7. On the night of December 16, 1773, about seventy men disguised as Mohawk Indians boarded three ships in Boston Harbor and destroyed 342 chests of tea valued at 10,000 pounds.

8. In 1774, the British Parliament passed four Coercive Acts that closed the port of Boston until residents paid for the destroyed tea. On September 1, 1774, the First Continental Congress met in Philadelphia to obtain repeal of the Coercive Acts and other restrictions.

9. The Virginia House of Burgesses was undecided about whether to take military action against the British. In Richmond, on March 23, 1775, **PATRICK HENRY** (1736–1799) ended his impassioned speech for action with those ringing words.

10. The battles of Lexington and Concord (Massachusetts) were fought on April 19, 1775. British troops, led by

GENERAL THOMAS GAGE, killed forty-nine militiamen and wounded forty-three. British losses totaled seventy-three dead and two hundred wounded.

11. "The shot heard 'round the world" first appeared in **RALPH WALDO EMERSON**'s poem "Concord Hymn" (1837). It refers to the Battle of Concord, Massachusetts, which, with the Battle of Lexington, ignited the Revolution.

12. Poet **HENRY WADSWORTH LONGFELLOW** composed "Paul Revere's Ride" in 1860 to commemorate the battles of Lexington and Concord, and the start of the American War for Independence.

13. PAUL REVERE (1735–1818) rode from Boston to Lexington to warn that the British were moving on Lexington to arrest John Hancock and Samuel Adams and on Concord to seize an arsenal there (which had already been removed and hidden). Revere was arrested, with **WILLIAM DAWES** and **SAMUEL PRESCOTT**. Dawes and Prescott escaped, and Dawes eventually reached Concord. Revere was held for several hours. Finally, the soldiers released him and left him to walk home.

14. The minutemen were a small, elite force, about one-quarter of the American militia, handpicked for their youth, strength, and speed of response ("ready in a minute") to any threat of foreign invasion.

15. The British garrison on Lake Champlain in upstate New York fell to **ETHAN ALLEN** (1738–1789) and his Green Mountain Boys of Vermont. The Green Mountain Boys were a local militia originally organized to drive New York settlers out of the area that later became Vermont.

16. Seeking to make the revolution an American war and not just a New England war, the Congress appointed **GEORGE WASHINGTON** of Virginia as commander-in-chief of the Continental army.

17. On June 17, 1775, the so-called Battle of Bunker Hill actually took place on and around the adjacent Breed's Hill, above Charlestown, near Boston. The British won the engagement when the rebels' ammunition ran out.

18. The British suffered crushing losses, with more than a thousand killed or wounded, many of them officers. The

Americans learned that their relatively inexperienced forces could stand up to regular troops in a pitched battle.

19. On January 10, 1776, **THOMAS PAINE** (1737–1809) published *Common Sense*, which argued for colonial independence from England. The thin pamphlet sold more than half a million copies in its first year.

20. At the darkest time of the Revolutionary War, Washington and his 11,000 to 12,000 men hunkered down in Valley Forge, twenty miles northwest of Philadelphia. Thousands died or deserted during the winter. Many others were severely ill. This was one of the most difficult times of the revolution for the American patriots.

21. GENERAL BENEDICT ARNOLD (1741–1801) planned to surrender the fort at West Point, New York, which he commanded, to the British. The plot was exposed in 1780. Arnold defected and became a brigadier general in the British army.

22. Lafayette served with great distinction as a general at the battles of Brandywine, Rhode Island, and Yorktown, and helped rally additional French support for the American cause. He became known as the "Hero of the Two Worlds."

23. GEORGE WASHINGTON could have become a king or dictator. His resignation established civilian authority over military authority and fortified the republican foundations of our new nation.

24. Independence Hall in Philadelphia and Monticello, the home of Thomas Jefferson in Virginia, are UNESCO World Heritage Sites.

25. The Americans licked the British. 😀

26. Tea-shirts. 😀

27. He found them revolting. 😀

28. Chicken catch-a-Tory. 😀

29. The herd shot 'round the world. 😀

30. Laughayette. 😀

31. Rudolph the Redcoat Reindeer. 😀

STAR-SPANGLED
SONGS

★ ★ ★ ★

ULYSSES S. GRANT once quipped, "I know only two tunes. One of them is 'Yankee Doodle,' and the other isn't."

Americans love to sing about their country. Most of us know the tune and at least the opening lyrics to the likes of "Hail, Columbia," "Dixie," "Battle Hymn of the Republic," "When Johnny Comes Marching Home Again," "Stars and Stripes Forever," and "You're a Grand Old Flag."

1 "Yankee Doodle" was America's unofficial national anthem until it was replaced by "The Star-Spangled Banner." The first verse runs:

Yankee Doodle went to town,
Riding on a pony.
He stuck a feather in his hat
And called it macaroni.

What are the origins of the words *Yankee, doodle,* and *macaroni*?

2 Despite the insults in its lyrics, what reaction did the colonists have to "Yankee Doodle"?

3 Who wrote the words to "The Star-Spangled Banner"?

4 What battle inspired amateur poet **FRANCIS SCOTT KEY** (1779–1843) to write his poem?

5 In September 1814, the British Navy furiously shelled Fort McHenry, killing four Americans and wounding twenty-four. What was the outcome of that battle?

6 What was the original title of the poem **FRANCIS SCOTT KEY** wrote?

7 Francis Scott Key wrote about "the broad stripes and bright stars" that bedecked the colossal flag that flew over Fort McHenry. How many stripes and stars were on that flag?

8 Where can you see the flag that waved over Fort McHenry?

9 What is the source of the music that accompanies "The Star-Spangled Banner"?

10 When did "The Star-Spangled Banner" become our official national anthem?

11 What is the origin of the motto "In God We Trust"?

12 Who wrote the words to the soaring song "America the Beautiful"?

13 Who wrote "God Bless America"?

Answers

1. The original Yankees were Dutch settlers who had come to the new world, and *Yankee* may derive from the Dutch *Jan Kaas,* meaning "Johnny Cheese." *Yankee* migrated from an ethnic insult against the Dutch to New Englanders in general when the song began life as a pre-Revolutionary creation originally sung by British military officers. The intent of "Yankee Doodle" was to mock the rag-tag, disorganized New Englanders with whom the British served in the French and Indian War.

Doodle first appeared in the early seventeenth century and derives from the Low German word *dudel,* meaning "fool" or "simpleton." The *macaroni* wig was in high fashion in the 1770s and became contemporary slang for foppishness. The last two lines of the verse implied that the unsophisticated Yankee bumpkins thought that simply sticking a feather in a cap would make them the height of fashion.

2. The colonists liked the tune of "Yankee Doodle" and adopted it as a robust marching song. What was once a derisive musical ditty became a source of American pride.

3. **FRANCIS SCOTT KEY**, a thirty-five-year-old attorney who tried to negotiate the freedom of a friend held hostage by the British during the War of 1812, wrote the words to what is now called "The Star-Spangled Banner." They were first published on September 20, 1814.

4. On September 13 and 14, 1814, the British attempted to capture Baltimore Harbor by taking Fort McHenry, which would have effectively split the United States in half.

5. When the sun rose after the battle, **FRANCIS SCOTT KEY** saw, to his joy, that a colossal American flag still waved. The battle for control of Baltimore was over, and the Americans had won.

6. Key expressed his emotions in a poem that he wrote on the back of an envelope. Titled "Defence of Fort M'Henry," those verses were later renamed "The Star-Spangled Banner."

7. The flag that Key watched displayed fifteen stars and fifteen stripes, representing the original thirteen states plus Vermont (1791) and Kentucky (1792).

8. That flag is on display at the Smithsonian Institution's National Museum of American History in Washington, D.C. After all the rockets' red glare and bombs bursting in air, it's riddled with eleven holes.

9. The poem was set to the tune of a British drinking song, "To Anacreon in Heaven," and was published in 1814 in Baltimore. It became popular immediately.

10. Later than you might think. It was not until March 3, 1931, that "The Star-Spangled Banner" was made our official national anthem by a congressional resolution signed by **PRESIDENT HERBERT HOOVER**.

11. The motto appears to be adapted from a line in the fourth stanza of **FRANCIS SCOTT KEY**'s "The Star-Spangled Banner": "And this be our motto—'In God is our Trust.'"

12. The lyrics to "America the Beautiful" were written by **KATHERINE LEE BATES** (1859–1929), a professor of English literature at Wellesley College. While teaching in Colorado in the summer of 1893, she was inspired to write her poem by a view from Pikes Peak. Although Bates never met New Jersey church organist **SAMUEL A. WARD**, the music of his hymn "Materna," composed in 1882, was combined with Bates's poem. The two were first published together in 1910.

13. Composer and lyricist **IRVING BERLIN** wrote "God Bless America" in 1918. Berlin created the song for a revue of his titled *Yip Yip Yaphank,* but he set it aside because he believed that the piece was too solemn for his otherwise comedic show. Twenty years later, as the shadow of Adolf Hitler rose to darken the world, Berlin, a Jewish immigrant born in the Russian Empire, decided to revise his handiwork from a victory song to a peace song. "God Bless America" was introduced and sung by **KATE SMITH** on a 1938 Armistice Day radio broadcast, backed by full orchestra and chorus. It became an instant hit.

STATES

★ ★ ★ ★

Of our fifty states, which is the most northerly, which the most westerly, which the most easterly, and which the most southerly?

The answers are **ALASKA, ALASKA, ALASKA,** and **HAWAII.** Here's why: Hawaii is more southerly than Florida, and Alaska is clearly our most northerly state. The Aleutian Islands, which are part of Alaska, arc about 1,110 miles west of the Alaskan Peninsula and cross the 180th meridian—the dividing line between the Eastern and Western hemispheres. That makes Alaska the state that's not just farthest north, but also the farthest west and farthest east.

Here's a stately quiz about our states.

1 Of our fifty states, which is the largest?

2 Name our two most populous states.

3 Identify seven states that are named after European kings and queens.

4 Which state is named after a president?

5 Was **NEW MEXICO** named for the country of Mexico?

6 Which state is known as the "Birthplace of Presidents"?

7 Which state is known as the "Mother of Presidents"?

8 **UNDER WHAT CIRCUMSTANCES DID WEST VIRGINIA BECOME A STATE ON JUNE 20, 1861?**

9 Who negotiated the **LOUISIANA PURCHASE**?

10 **IN 1867, SECRETARY OF STATE WILLIAM SEWARD WAS SCORNED FOR WHAT WAS CALLED "SEWARD'S FOLLY." WHAT WAS IT?**

11 Which states border the most other states? Which touches just one other state? Which states stand alone?

12 What did Delaware? 🙂

13 What did Tennessee? 🙂

14 What state wears glasses? 🙂

15 What is the smartest state? 🙂

Answers

1. Seventy-five New Jerseys could fit into **ALASKA**. Alaska is not only our largest state, but is larger than the second and third largest states—**TEXAS** and **CALIFORNIA**—combined. Taken together, these three states make up more than a quarter of our nation's total acreage.

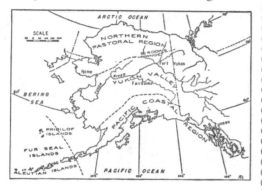

2. One out of eight of us lives in **CALIFORNIA**; the second most populous state is **TEXAS**. These states will continue to attract people as the mean center of U.S. population shifts southward and westward. The 2010 mean center of population is near the village of **PLATO** in **TEXAS COUNTY, MISSOURI**. That center moved 23.4 miles southwest of where it had been in the year 2000.

3. **NORTH** and **SOUTH CAROLINA** (King Charles I of England), **GEORGIA** (King George II of England), **LOUISIANA** (King Louis IV of France), **VIRGINIA** and **WEST VIRGINIA** (Queen Elizabeth I of England, who was known as the Virgin Queen), and **MARYLAND** (Queen Henrietta Maria, wife of Charles I).

4. **WASHINGTON** is the only state named after a president.

5. Nuevo (New) México was named in 1563 for the Mexica (Aztec) empire. Nuevo España (New Spain) was renamed Mexico in 1821.

6. **VIRGINIA** is the birth state of the greatest number of our presidents, including four of the first five and seven of the first twelve: George Washington, Thomas Jefferson, James Madison, James Monroe, William Henry Harrison, John Tyler, and Zachary Taylor, as well as twentieth-century president Woodrow Wilson. Jefferson, Monroe, and Tyler were also governors of Virginia.

7. In competition with Virginia, **OHIO** is known as the "Mother of Presidents" because seven American presidents were born there: Ulysses S. Grant, Rutherford B. Hayes, James Garfield (Grant, Hayes, and Garfield served consecutively), Benjamin Harrison, William McKinley, William Howard Taft, and Warren G. Harding. William Henry Harrison lived there at the time of his election.

8. Its political leaders were opposed to **VIRGINIA**'s decision to secede from the Union, so **WEST VIRGINIA** broke from the Confederacy and was admitted to the Union as a separate state.

Negotiating the Louisiana Purchase

9. The **LOUISIANA PURCHASE** was negotiated in 1803 by James Monroe and Robert Livingston, who were then Thomas Jefferson's diplomats to France. Although Monroe later became president of the United States, he always considered the Purchase to be his greatest achievement.

10. Seward arranged the purchase of **ALASKA** from Russia for $7.2 million. At 586,412 square miles, the price worked out to about two cents per acre. It had a population of 60,000–70,000, mostly indigenous.

11. The states that border the most other states—eight—are **TENNESSEE** and **MISSOURI**. **MAINE** is the only state that touches just one other state, **NEW HAMPSHIRE**. Only **ALASKA** and **HAWAII** stand alone.

12. She wore a New Jersey. 😊

13. She saw what Arkansas. 😊

14. Mississippi. It has four *i*'s. 😊

15. Alabama. It has four *a*'s and a *b*. 😊

THE
WHITE
HOUSE

What is now called the White House was originally called the President's House, the Presidential Mansion, or the Executive Mansion. Ironically, the only president who didn't live in Washington was . . . Washington. During **GEORGE WASHINGTON**'s administration the nation's capital was situated in New York and later Philadelphia.

1 What is the address of the White House?

2 Who was the first president to live in the Executive Mansion?

3 Construction of the White House was completed in 1800. Why did it need to be rebuilt in 1814?

4 Electric lights were probably first used on a Christmas tree in 1882. When was the White House Christmas tree first adorned with electric lights?

5 Which president proclaimed the "White House" as the official name of his residence?

Answers

1. The address is 1600 Pennsylvania Avenue. Pennsylvania Avenue, used for many parades and demonstrations, connects the White House to the U.S. Capitol 1.2 miles away. A total of 5.8 miles long, it was laid out by **PIERRE CHARLES L'ENFANT** (1754–1825) in his overall design for Washington. It was first mentioned in a letter from **THOMAS JEFFERSON** in 1791, but it wasn't paved until 1832. Dust was a constant irritant.

Pierre L'Enfant's plan for Washington, 1792

2. It was **JOHN ADAMS** who first occupied what was then known as the President's House. He moved into the building on November 1, 1800, while the paint was still drying. His wife, Abigail, joined him later in the month. They lived there for only four months, having lived most of the presidential term in Philadelphia.

3. On August 24, 1814, during the War of 1812, British troops burned the White House, the Capitol, and other public buildings. Rebuilding took until 1817.

4. Electricity was installed in the White House in 1891. Tree lights came in 1895 during **GROVER CLEVELAND**'s presidency. The first ad for tree lights appeared in 1900 in *Scientific American.* They were so expensive, people rented them.

5. THEODORE ROOSEVELT declared by presidential proclamation in 1901 that the Executive Mansion should henceforth be known as the "White House." It was called the White House from when construction was completed and its sandstone walls were whitewashed, but Roosevelt was the first to use that term on presidential stationery.

WRITERS

On the night of April 20, 1910, Halley's Comet shone in the skies as it made its closest approach to the Earth. Just a year before, **MARK TWAIN** said to a friend, "I came in with Halley's Comet in 1835. It is coming again next year, and I expect to go out with it. . . . The almighty has said, no doubt, 'Now here go these two unaccountable frauds; they came in together, they must go out together.' Oh! I am looking forward to that." On April 21, 1910, Mark Twain, the most American of American writers, did indeed go out with Halley's Comet.

HENRY DAVID THOREAU (1817–1862), who wrote *Walden,* helped runaway slaves escape to Canada and became one of the first Americans to speak in defense of radical abolitionist and outlaw John Brown. When Thoreau spent a day in jail for acting on the dictates of his conscience, he was visited by friend **RALPH WALDO EMERSON** (1803–1882).

Emerson asked, "Henry, why are you here?"

Thoreau answered, "Waldo, why are you *not* here?"

Through biographical incidents, we can sometimes catch and crystallize the essence of a person's character. Here are some revealing episodes from the lives of ten famous American authors, each of whom you are asked to identify.

1 When the first edition of this poet's collection of poems appeared in 1855, the *Boston Intelligencer* said in its review: "The author should be kicked out from all decent society as below the level of the brute. He must be some escaped lunatic raving in pitiable delirium." The collection went through nine more editions and gained a large, enthusiastic readership in the United States and England.

Lived at Walden Pond for two years

2 Only seven of this reclusive New England woman's poems were published during her lifetime, and she left instructions that all her manuscripts be destroyed. Fortunately, they survived. Today, she and her contemporary in the question above are the two most widely read and influential American poets of the nineteenth century.

3 This writer, critic, and humorist once arrived simultaneously at a narrow doorway with the playwright, journalist, and politician **CLARE BOOTHE LUCE.**

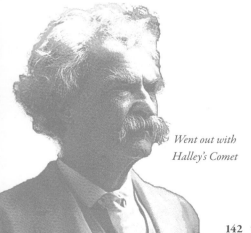

Went out with Halley's Comet

"Age before beauty," said Mrs. Luce, stepping aside.

"Pearls before swine," purred our writer as she glided through the doorway.

4 His epitaph reads, "Quoth the Raven, 'Nevermore,'" a line in his most famous poem.

5 When a popular Jazz Age novelist remarked to another famous writer that "the rich are very different from you and me," the latter replied, "Yes, they have more money." Name the two authors.

Reclusive New England poet

6 When he was a young busboy in a Washington, D.C., hotel, this poet left a packet of his poems next to the poet **VACHEL LINDSAY**'s plate. Lindsay helped to launch the young man's career, and the busboy became the leading figure in the Harlem Renaissance.

7 In 1900, this author sat down to write a children's book about a girl named Dorothy, who was swept away to a fantastic land. The fairy tale began as a

Popular Jazz Age American novelist

bedtime story for the author's children and their friends and soon spilled over into several evening sessions. During one of the tellings, the author was asked the name of the strange place to which Dorothy was swept away. Glancing about the room, his eyes fell upon the drawers of a filing cabinet labeled "A–N" and "O–Z." Noting that the letters on the second label spelled out the *ah*s uttered by his rapt listeners, he named his fantastic land Oz.

8 This reclusive writer was depicted in W. P. Kinsella's 1982 novel *Shoeless Joe.* When the subject threatened to sue, he was replaced in the film version, titled *Field of Dreams,* by a fictitious writer named Terence Mann, portrayed by James Earl Jones.

9 This poet was asked to compose a poem and read it at John F. Kennedy's inauguration in 1961. When the sun's glare prevented him from reading the poem at the occasion, he instead recited his poem "The Gift Outright" from memory.

10 The publishers of the children's classic *Charlotte's Web* persuaded its author to record his book on tape. So caught had he become in the web of his arachnid heroine's life that it took nineteen tapings before the author could read aloud the passage about Charlotte's death without his voice cracking.

Answers

1. **WALT WHITMAN** (1819–1892)
2. **EMILY DICKINSON** (1830–1886)
3. **DOROTHY PARKER** (1893–1967)
4. **EDGAR ALLAN POE** (1809–1849)
5. **F. SCOTT FITZGERALD** (1896–1940) and **ERNEST HEMINGWAY** (1899–1961)
6. **LANGSTON HUGHES** (1902–1967)
7. **L. FRANK BAUM** (1856–1919)
8. **J. D. SALINGER** (1919–2010)
9. **ROBERT FROST** (1874–1963)
10. **E. B. WHITE** (1899–1985)